WORLD RELIGIONS A BEGINNER'S GUIDE

WORLD
RELIGIONS
A BEGINNER'S GUIDE

QUESTIONS AND ANSWERS
FOR HUMANITY'S
7 OLDEST AND LARGEST FAITHS

Jill Carroll, PhD

ROCKRIDGE
PRESS

For general information on our other products and services or to obtain technical support, please contact our Customer Care Department within the United States at (866) 744-2665, or outside the United States at (510) 253-0500.

Rockridge Press publishes its books in a variety of electronic and print formats. Some content that appears in print may not be available in electronic books, and vice versa.

Interior and Cover Designer: Julie Schrader
Art Producer: Hannah Dickerson
Editor: Adrian Potts
Production Editor: Ashley Polikoff

All images used under license from iStock.com

ISBN: Print 978-1-64876-914-6 | eBook 978-1-64876-915-3
R0

For everyone who has ever felt misunderstood because of their religion, and in the hope that together we can create a world of peaceful coexistence for people of all faiths and no faith.

CONTENTS

Introduction ix

Chapter One: Hinduism 1

Chapter Two: Judaism 23

Chapter Three: Taoism 47

Chapter Four: Buddhism 71

Chapter Five: Christianity 95

Chapter Six: Islam 121

Chapter Seven: Sikhism 145

Further Reading 167

References 168

Index 170

INTRODUCTION

For nearly as long as we humans have been on Earth, we have created, practiced, and participated in forms of religion. Religion is one of the primary ways that we ask and answer the deepest, most enduring questions about human existence: *Who are we? Why are we here? How did we get here? How should we live? What happens when we die?*

But religions are more than just a way to answer questions about life; they also impact every corner of our cultures. Religions have inspired some of the best and most significant art, architecture, literature, philosophy, and theology. The world's great religions have also brought our attention to some of the most fascinating, inspiring people who have ever lived—people who founded religious practices or lived as saints or sages.

For all these reasons and more, studying the world's great religions isn't just a way to learn more about different spiritual practices. It's also a way to better understand humanity as a whole.

What Is the Purpose of This Book?

This book is designed to give you a basic understanding of the world's oldest and most popular religions: Hinduism, Judaism, Taoism, Buddhism, Christianity, Islam, and Sikhism. It will examine the core history, concepts, figures, practices, and texts of each of these religions, answering your most pressing questions and introducing you to information that you might not already know.

It will also show you the connective tissue between these religions—how they are related to one another historically and which basic ideas and concepts they share.

This book will *not* exhaustively cover each religion in all its myriad forms, permutations, people, gods, teachings, rituals, and other aspects. Rather, it will explain these religions in their most classic and traditional forms—forms that might not match up with every practitioner's experience of them. All religions have lots of diversity within them, and the people who practice religion do so in ways that are unique to them. No two Christians, Hindus, Muslims, or members of any religion are the same!

Moreover, religions interact with other aspects of human culture in complex and nuanced ways. Sometimes religions offer critiques of existing cultural traditions—like norms for gender roles, family structures, economic systems, and so on—and encourage people to adopt new and different cultural patterns and beliefs. Other times, religions blend with existing cultural traditions without changing them much at all.

And sometimes a religion will do both, depending on the time and place. In short, religions and the cultures they are a part of are delightfully messy and complicated and can look all sorts of ways across the world.

So, this book is not an encyclopedia of religions. It is a way to learn the basic and most readily identifiable ways these major religions show up in the world. If you're interested, you can learn more and move into a deeper understanding of the nuances and complexities within each of these religions. This book will set you up well to branch off into learning whatever captures your imagination about these amazing, fascinating faiths.

What Makes a Religion a Religion?

So, what *is* a religion? What makes something a religion, as opposed to simply a philosophy or a worldview? Why is Christianity, for example, a religion, while Kantianism (the ideas of German philosopher Immanuel Kant) is a philosophy?

Scholars of religion differ on what exactly defines a religion, but most of them agree with scholar Rudolf Otto, who says that religions are focused on "the holy." The idea of holiness plays a role in religions that it doesn't play in organized philosophies or other belief systems. In each religion, whatever is considered holy is seen as the most ultimate reality, the greatest value, the deepest truth or force in existence, and the thing that defines meaning for everything. The holy may be a deity, such as the singular God of Judaism, Christianity, and

Islam. The holy can also be the many gods of Hinduism, which express different faces of the one divine reality. The holy could be a primal force or energy, like the Tao in Taoism. The holy can even be a state of consciousness, such as enlightenment or nirvana in Buddhism and Hinduism. (Don't worry if you don't know what any of these terms mean—they are explored later in the book.)

No matter what a specific religion defines as holy, the holy sits at the center of it. It informs everything the people of that religion do when they engage with the beliefs and practices of their faith. All of the religions covered in this book contain a clear idea of the holy and offer the people who practice them many ways to understand, seek, and experience the holy in their own lives. Formal ways of engaging with the holy include attending services at a mosque, synagogue, or other house of worship; practicing rituals mediated by priests or other clergy; or saying preset prayers alone or with a group. Informal ways of encountering the holy include reading sacred texts during private devotionals at home or seeking out a divine presence as you walk along a beach or in a beautiful forest.

Indeed, one reason humans form religions in the first place is to try to explain their own experiences of the holy—experiences with something not mundane, something seemingly beyond the everyday, and something that seemed more true, more real, more powerful, and more awe-inspiring than anything else. A person saw a bright light, or heard a voice, or gained a powerful insight, or saw a vision, or had an out-of-body experience, and it fundamentally changed their life forever. And the religion they started as a result of this encounter with the holy ended up changing the whole world.

Why Focus on These Seven Religions?

The seven religions we'll cover in this book were not chosen because they are the most "true," the "best," or the "most important" religions of all time. Rather, they were chosen because they have existed in an organized form for a very long time, and because, due to their histories and large number of followers, they have been the most influential and widespread in the world's cultures.

For example, it is impossible to understand India's history and culture without understanding Hinduism, as the religion has shaped nearly every aspect of India's culture from its inception 4,000 years ago to this very moment. Likewise, Christianity, as a belief system that blended with various empires in Europe and elsewhere, has wielded incredible influence on the history, politics, cultures, and even the geography of what is often called "the West." The same could be said of Islam, which has existed not only as a religion but also as a part of powerful empires like the Ottoman and the Mughal, which shaped world history for several centuries. In short, this book covers the religions that have been and remain some of the most dominant forces in human culture and life.

That doesn't mean the religions not included in this book aren't important or influential; they certainly are. Confucianism, for example, has deeply shaped Chinese culture from its inception in the 5th century BCE through the rise of Chairman Mao in the 20th century CE. Jainism—especially the religion's philosophy of *ahimsa*, or noninjury—is widely influential. Baha'i, Shinto, Zoroastrianism, and many others not addressed directly here are amazing religions that are every bit as fascinating as the ones covered in this book. Some of these religions will be touched on in other chapters—for instance, Confucianism will be discussed in the chapter about Taoism (see page 47). But even the religions not addressed in this book at all are fascinating, and studying them will give you more insight into human existence.

How to Use This Book

This book is designed for beginners—folks who may have heard of the religions listed here but know very little or nothing about them. If this is you, then welcome!

This book is set up so that you can read it from start to finish, or you can hop around based on what piques your interest. Each chapter is designed to be freestanding, so you don't have to read the previous chapter for it to make sense. The religions are arranged chronologically, from oldest to newest, so if you read the book from front to back, you will get a sense of the history of religion.

Additionally, the "Further Reading" section (page 167) provides resources you may use to continue your learning and go deeper into some of the basic concepts introduced in this book.

Finally, the whole book is written in an informal, everyday tone, intended to convey information in the simplest, clearest ways possible. You won't get bogged down in stodgy academic writing or endless encyclopedic details. Instead, this book is organized around the most important facts and some of the most commonly asked questions about each religion. May this book be the beginning of an incredible and joyful journey of discovery for you.

THE "OM" SYMBOL, PAGE 19

CHAPTER ONE

Hinduism

Hinduism was founded about 4,000 years ago, making it one of the oldest religions in the world. It's also one of the largest, with over 1 billion adherents. It began in India and remains dominant there, but it is also practiced throughout the world. Additionally, it is the parent religion to Buddhism, so the two religions share a number of central ideas, including karma and reincarnation.

Hinduism is very diverse and offers many different ways to practice its main tenets and rituals. Hinduism is also a beautiful and colorful religion, sometimes quite literally! Many Hindu temples have gorgeous interiors filled with intricate paintings and statues, and many Hindu rituals involve sumptuous foods, garlands of flowers, chanting, festive lights, and even throwing colored powders on people.

Hinduism offers a perfect example of how religions stay vibrant and alive over time: *They evolve.* Religions are not static or fixed; they are living, dynamic systems that seek to meet people's needs in every historical moment. Hinduism has been a vital part of Indian spirituality for thousands of years because of its adaptability and richness. As such, it's the perfect religion for us to start with.

Cheat Sheet

When it began: around 4,000 years ago

Number of adherents: over 1 billion

Percentage of world population: about 15 percent

Primary location: India

Largest sect/denomination: the Vedanta school of thought

Primary texts: the *Vedas*, the *Upanishads*, the *Mahabharata* (which contains the *Bhagavad Gita*), the *Ramayana*, and many others

Most recognizable symbol: the "om" or "aum" symbol (page xvi), also the *bindu* or *bindi*— a small dot worn on the forehead

KEY DATES

3300– 1300 BCE	Indus Valley Civilization (also called Harappan Civilization after its major city) develops. It is a major founding source of what later became Hindu religion.
1500– 1200 BCE	Aryan (Indo-European) people enter the Indian subcontinent, bringing Sanskrit language and other religio-cultural ideas that become part of Hinduism.
1500– 500 BCE	Vedic period: the four main collections of the *Vedas* (*Rig Veda*, *Sama Veda*, *Yajur Veda*, and *Atharva Veda*) are written.
800– 200 BCE	The major *Upanishads* (commentaries on the *Vedas*) are written.
400 BCE– 400 CE	Major Hindu epics *Mahabharata* and *Ramayana* are composed.
200 BCE– 200 CE	*Laws of Manu* (*Manusmriti*), an influential document and code of traditions, laws, duties, rights, rules, and virtues, are composed and codified.
320– 550 CE	Gupta Empire: known for its prosperity, scientific discovery, and achievements in arts and language. Much of Hindu life and practice becomes stabilized and extended throughout the subcontinent.
700	Birth of Adi Sankaracharya (or simply Sankara), the highly influential Indian philosopher and theologian of the Vedanta school of thought, a dominant form of Hinduism.
1526–1761	Mughal Empire: a Persian Muslim dynasty that governed northern India.
1617	The British East India Company is granted trading rights by the Mughals. As the empire declines, the company's importance and influence grows.
1858	India comes under direct rule of the British crown.
1869	Birth of Mohandas Gandhi—lawyer, activist, politician, reformer, and spiritual leader instrumental in achieving Indian independence from Britain. Gandhi was assassinated in 1948.
1947	India achieves independence from Britain. As part of Britain's pullout, northern India is partitioned into a separate state called Pakistan.

On the Hindu Calendar

MAHA SHIVARATRI

February or March

Known as "Shiva's Great Night," this festival honors the grand marriage between the god Shiva with the goddess Parvati. It features fasting, prayers, and colorful processions.

KUMBH MELA

February or March

Kumbh Mela, which is celebrated in a 12-year cycle, honors a story in which divine nectar dripped out of vessels being carried by demons in flight from the gods. Every three years, it is celebrated in one of four sacred cities (the sites where the nectar drops fell). The celebration in the sacred city of Prayag, which occurs once every 12 years, is particularly auspicious because of astrological conjunctions, and it is one of the largest religious gatherings in the world.

HOLI

March

Holi is the "Festival of Color," a springtime festival that commemorates the triumph of good over evil—namely, the burning of a demoness named Holika. A favorite festival among children, its celebrations include participants throwing colored powders and water on one another.

NAVARATRI

September or October

Navaratri—which translates to "nine nights" and is also celebrated as Durga Puja in some parts of India—is a festival dedicated to the mother goddess Durga. Celebrated on the fall equinox, it honors Durga's slaying of a buffalo demon, which also testifies to the power of good to defeat the forces of evil. Some nights of the festival honor other goddesses in addition to Durga.

DIWALI

October or November

Known as the "Festival of Lights," Diwali marks the victory of light over darkness and good over evil. Celebrated on the new moon between October and November, it commemorates the deity Rama's return from exile. His path out of exile was lit by candles, so during Diwali, people put up string lights, light candles, and set off fireworks. Diwali is also celebrated by Jains and Sikhs, although with slightly different beliefs attached to it.

Burning Questions

WHO FOUNDED HINDUISM?

Hinduism is one of the few religions with no known founder. Instead, it began as a confluence of the religious practices of the ancient Indus River Valley Civilization and those of Indo-European people (called

Aryans) who came into northern India during the 2nd century BCE. Eventually, over centuries, the beliefs, practices, texts, and rituals that emerged from this confluence became known as Hinduism.

WHO ARE THE MOST IMPORTANT FIGURES WITHIN HINDUISM?

There are dozens of important figures throughout the long history of Hinduism. Chief among them are Patanjali, a great sage who is estimated to have lived sometime between the 2nd and 4th centuries CE and is credited with developing the dominant system of Hindu yoga; Sankara, an 8th-century scholar of the Vedanta school of thought; Ramakrishna, an influential 19th-century Hindu mystic; Vivekananda, a student of Ramakrishna who is largely responsible for bringing Hindu ideas to the Western world; and Gandhi, a reformer and political activist who helped India achieve independence from Britain and who influenced Dr. Martin Luther King Jr.'s ideas about passive, nonviolent resistance.

WHAT IS KARMA?

Karma is a dominant concept in Hinduism and other religions that began in India, including Buddhism, Jainism, and Sikhism. In a nutshell, karma is the idea that every human action, especially a morally significant one, has an energy that accompanies it and attaches to the person who performed the action. This energy can be either positive or negative, depending on the nature of the action. Thus, evil actions bring negative karma, and good actions bring positive karma. Positive karma can dissolve or cancel out negative karma. As long as a person has negative karma attached to them—either from their own actions or from actions from previous lives—they remain stuck in a cycle of life, death, and rebirth.

WHAT IS REINCARNATION?

Like karma, reincarnation is a central Hindu concept that also appears in Buddhism and Jainism. In short, reincarnation is a cyclical view of time in which individual souls (called *atman*) are reborn again and again until, through their own spiritual practice, they achieve *moksha,* or release from the cycle of life, death, and rebirth. When moksha—which translates to "release"— is achieved, the soul is released from the cycle of samsara, at which point the atman remerges with Brahman (the world soul).

Karma is one of the factors that determines the type of rebirth one will have in future lives. Hinduism, as well as all other religions that affirm karma and reincarnation, exhort people to make the most of their human life and make as much progress on the spiritual path as possible in order to escape the cycle of reincarnation and all the suffering that comes with it.

DO HINDUS WORSHIP MANY GODS?

Yes and no. Strictly speaking, there are many dozens of named Hindu gods and goddesses who are worshipped wherever Hinduism is practiced. Statues and pictures of them adorn temples, homes, stores, schools, and bill-boards, as well as print and digital media, all over India. Each god is known for having specific powers or abilities and is associated with certain symbols or elements, such as specific weapons, tools, animals, postures, clothing, and colors. Distinct sets of stories are told about every god.

At the same time, many Hindus will affirm that there really is only one divine reality, or one god, and will even claim to be monotheistic (believing in only one god, like Judaism or Islam). In this view, the many dozens of gods worshipped throughout Hinduism are really just facets or aspects of the one divine reality. Just as a cut diamond is only one stone but has different faces that reflect the light differently, each of the Hindu gods reflects a particular aspect or "face" of the one primal divine reality.

DOES THIS ONE PRIMAL DIVINE REALITY HAVE A NAME?

Usually it is called Brahman, which loosely translates to "the world soul." It is the primal essence and life of all existence, of the entire cosmos. Every individual soul or atman that exists—you, me, dogs, cats, fish, and so on—emerges from Brahman and will return to Brahman when it ceases being reincarnated into individual beings. All things come from and will return to Brahman.

A common analogy is of an endless ocean. Through evaporation, moisture is taken up from the ocean into the atmosphere, where it eventually becomes individual raindrops that fall through the sky for a time, only to finally merge back into the endless ocean. In this metaphor, all individual souls are but pieces of the world soul that become individualized "raindrops" for a time, before merging back into the world soul. Put more mystically, each one of us contains a spark of divinity inside us. This is a central teaching of the most dominant schools of thought in Hinduism.

IS THE SPIRITUAL GOAL IN HINDUISM TO MERGE BACK INTO BRAHMAN?

Yes, that's the ultimate goal. As noted in the explanation of reincarnation (page 7), this goal includes being released from the cycle of life, death, and rebirth. That release is called moksha, and the cycle is called samsara. Once moksha is attained—through all sorts of spiritual, meditative, ethical, and behavioral practices—samsara ceases, and the atman enters into union with Brahman. All spiritual practices in Hinduism are designed to help nullify negative karma and accrue positive karma in order to attain moksha and union with the divine.

WHAT ARE THE MOST IMPORTANT SPIRITUAL PRACTICES IN HINDUISM?

Hinduism includes a vast array of spiritual practices, but they can generally be broken down into three main groups or spiritual paths—the path of action, the path of knowledge, and the path of devotion. The path of action involves performing proper rituals, observing

holy days, and fulfilling one's duty in society. Traditionally, this path has included family and caste obligations,
although these have evolved in modern times and are
not as common among less traditional practitioners. The
path of knowledge includes all the meditative and schol-
arly practices that increase wisdom and expand one's
consciousness of the divine. And the path of devotion
focuses primarily on worship of and devotion to particular deities, as well as cultivating whatever virtues
each deity embodies or champions. None of these paths
is considered better than the other, and many observant Hindus practice aspects of all three of them in their
daily lives.

WHO ARE THE MOST IMPORTANT
GODS IN HINDUISM?

There is no official hierarchy of gods in Hinduism; no
one god is more important than all the others. That
said, there are gods who are more common or popular
than others within the vast landscape of Hinduism. The
most popular gods are the ones you would most likely
see if you visit a Hindu temple or encounter an altar in
the home of a Hindu friend. These gods include Shiva,
the god of creation and destruction, often depicted as
dancing in a ring of fire; Vishnu, the god who upholds
the cosmos and defends righteousness, often depicted
with skin the same light blue shade as the sky; Devi/
Durga, the great goddess who is the enlivening power
of the universe and is, in herself, the summation of
all goddesses (all other goddesses are essentially

Everyday Hinduism

Hinduism at Home

The most common form of religious practice for Hindus is a daily puja. This practice, which is usually done in the home, involves prayers and rituals oriented toward a specific god. A daily puja typically involves worshipping a particular Hindu god by singing chants, reading sacred texts, reciting prayers, making offerings of food or drink, and decorating the god's image or statue with flowers or jewelry. The puja may last from a few minutes to an hour or more, depending on the puja and the person.

Home altars used in puja can be simple or ornate and normally contain whatever utensils are necessary—bowls, trays, small ladles for sprinkling water, candles or small oil lamps, needle and thread for garlands, a small bell, and other such items. Pujas are acts of simple reverence for the god; they also serve as individual or household prayer requests for things like good health, safe travels, a happy marriage, success for one's children or spouse, or other such human wants.

a manifestation of her); Ganesha, Shiva's son, the elephant-headed god of writing who also removes obstacles; Krishna, one of several manifestations of Vishnu and the primary deity of the *Bhagavad Gita*; Lakshmi, Vishnu's consort and the goddess of good fortune and prosperity; Hanuman, the monkey god who appears in Hindu epic literature as a protector and helper; and Kali, the fierce goddess of disease, war, destruction, and time, often depicted wearing a garland of skulls.

WHAT ARE THE MOST IMPORTANT SACRED TEXTS IN HINDUISM?

Just as there are many gods in Hinduism, there are also many sacred texts. To get a handle on them, it helps to divide the texts into five groups: the *Vedas* (four collections), which are mainly hymns and rituals to the gods; the *Upanishads*, which are commentaries on the *Vedas*; the epic literature, which includes the *Ramayana* and the *Mahabharata* (which includes the *Bhagavad Gita*); the *Puranas*, a large collection of works championed by various sects that focus on legends of the gods, creation stories, explorations of how certain rituals or holy places became sacred, and so on; and the *Tantras*, a vast collection of esoteric and mystical texts that focus on the divine feminine and emphasize high-level spiritual practices. Of all these texts, the first three categories are the most prominent. Hindus revere the *Vedas* and *Upanishads* as containing the most ancient spiritual wisdom on the planet. Stories from the *Ramayana* and *Mahabharata* are enacted in street theater all over India, and people view the heroes of these stories as models of virtue and devotion.

WHAT KIND OF STORIES ARE TOLD IN THE MAHABHARATA AND RAMAYANA?

The *Mahabharata* is for Hindus what Homer's *Iliad* and *Odyssey* are for the Greeks; it tells of their history and of their heroes who achieved various types of glory. The *Mahabharata* tells of the great war between two sides of the same family. Throughout this massive text, the gods intervene by aiding or blocking the various human characters. The *Ramayana* tells of the travails and ultimate victory of the hero, Rama (who is revered as one of several manifestations of Vishnu), and his wife, Sita, as Rama is sent into exile for many years and Sita is abducted by a demon troll. Rama and Sita are valorized as the ideal married couple in Hinduism, each of them embodying the perfect man and woman.

IS THE CASTE SYSTEM PART OF HINDUISM?

Yes and no. Caste has traditionally been a societal duty on the path of action in spiritual life. The *Vedas* include a creation story in which the universe is created by the parts of a primal man who is sacrificed and dismembered by the gods. His mouth becomes the priestly caste, his arms become the warrior caste, his thighs become the merchant caste, and his feet become the servant caste. This story seems to indicate that the caste system is hardwired into the cosmos and part of the natural order. And for many centuries, this is exactly how caste was understood in Hinduism. People are born into a certain caste; they grow up, marry, and live their lives inside that caste, doing the work that is appropriate for their caste, and then if they do their caste duty well and accumulate good karma, they might be reborn into a higher caste.

However, generations of Hindu reformers have challenged this idea, pointing to the unfairness of it and to the ways in which it prompts people of higher castes to look down upon and feel superior to people of lower castes. Moreover, they suggest, stories like that of the primal man simply point out that societies naturally divide themselves into groups, not that those groups have to be fixed or that one's place in a caste must be permanent. Gandhi, for example, argued against most of the common caste restrictions of his day and shared meals and fellowship with people from lower castes. Discrimination based on caste has officially been illegal since 1950, when India adopted its constitution as an independent country. That said, caste sensibility is deeply engrained in Indian Hindu culture, so even though the law no longer upholds caste discrimination, it endures as a cultural perspective.

ARE ALL HINDUS VEGETARIAN?

No, but vegetarianism is exhorted as an ideal. While it's hard to find exact figures on what percentage of Hindus are vegetarian, it has been a strong feature of the religion, and of Indian culture in general, for hundreds of years. Jainism's teaching of ahimsa (noninjury) and its own strong exhortations to vegetarianism (even veganism, in many instances) have had a lasting influence on Hindu and Buddhist religious and dietary practices. However, government studies indicate that only about a quarter of the entire Indian population (which includes not only Hindus but also Muslims, Christians, Sikhs, Jains, and others) is vegetarian. Also, some Hindus who eat meat will still not eat beef because of the traditions regarding sacredness associated with cows.

SO WHY ARE COWS SACRED IN HINDUISM?

There are several reasons why Hindus hold cows as sacred, and although their origins are murky, they all swirl together to create a strong and enduring conviction to protect cows from slaughter and to honor them as special animals. Early Vedic literature tells of a goddess named Kamadhenu who is part human, part cow. She is a mother goddess of abundance whose very body provides nurture and nourishment. Additionally, stories of Krishna frolicking with the *gopis*, Sanskrit for "cowherd girls," lend themselves to associating cows with Krishna. Furthermore, Vishnu is often depicted in Hindu art alongside cows or in association with pastures, butter, milk, and other things related to cows. While it is unknown if cows became sacred because of their association with gods or because they were already seen as sacred, they are revered and protected as divine symbols of the bounty of Earth.

Everyday Hinduism

The True Roots of Yoga

The term "yoga" means "to unite," as well as "to discipline or train." Most Westerners think of yoga as a way to reduce stress and increase strength, agility, and mental clarity. But in Hinduism, yoga is a spiritual discipline of the body and mind designed to bring the self into spiritual union with the divine. What many in the West think of as yoga—the different physical postures and stretches accompanied by measured, focused breathing—is but one of several stages of a Hindu spiritual discipline attributed to a sage named Patanjali. Additionally, traditional Hindu medicine (called *Ayurvedic* medicine) views yoga's physical postures, known as *asanas*, as necessary for maintaining the body's health and energy centers.

WHAT ARE THE DIFFERENT GROUPS OR SECTS WITHIN HINDUISM?

There are many different schools of thought in Hinduism, and within each of these groups, there are multiple subgroups. There are also myriad sects in Hinduism that are oriented around certain sacred texts or specific interpretations of them. The two main groups within Hinduism, however, are the Vaishnavites and Shaivites.

Vaishnavites focus their religious energy on Vishnu, the preserver god who protects the cosmos from being destroyed. This group focuses on his manifestations, as well as any other gods or goddesses associated with him. There are several schools of thought within Vaishnavism, and each has a different understanding of the divine/human relationship, Vishnu's influence in the world, and Vishnu's incarnations and manifestations.

Shaivites, by contrast, focus on Shiva, the destroyer god, who creates and transforms the cosmos. Shaivites are also divided into subgroups who have different and specific understandings of the divine/human relationship, the practices that foster this relationship, and who Shiva is in relation to the cosmos.

WHAT KIND OF CLERGY OR RELIGIOUS LEADERSHIP DOES HINDUISM HAVE?

Hinduism doesn't have a central authority or hierarchy that doles out offices and titles in a uniform way throughout the entire religion. Instead, each sect, school of thought, or group within Hinduism determines its own leadership structures, decides who gets to lead, and chooses what to call those leaders. But in general, there are a handful of names or titles used for religious leaders that span the breadth of Hinduism.

The most common Hindu title is priest, who officiates the major rituals for major life events (i.e., birth, marriage, death, etc.) or the observances on the Hindu sacred calendar. Another title would be swami, which is used for spiritual teachers or scholars, like the 19th-century teacher and reformer Swami Vivekananda. A guru is also a spiritual teacher, particularly one with whom an individual studies, one-on-one or in small groups, for any length of time. Yogi refers to a person who has taken on the most austere spiritual disciplines and physical practices designed to attain union with Brahman. Yogis are people who have largely abandoned everyday household life and spend most of their time in deep meditation, chanting, holding the postures of yoga, fasting, and engaging in other exacting spiritual disciplines. Perhaps the most generic term is *sadhu*, which refers to any Hindu holy man, including any of those listed in this section.

IS GANDHI IMPORTANT TO HINDUS?

While Gandhi's legacy within India is complex, he is revered by many Hindus and non-Hindus alike for his political activism working toward achieving independence from Britain in the mid-20th century. Though he became world famous as a lawyer and political figure, his politics were rooted in his deep religious beliefs about nonviolence and the divinity of every human.

Gandhi's ideas on noninjury (which he learned as a young person from a Jain tutor) greatly influenced his political activism in the direction of passive, nonviolent resistance.

These ideas, famously, came to influence Christian pastor and activist Martin Luther King Jr. in his work to bring civil rights to African Americans in the United States. India achieved its independence without having to go to war with Britain, and many attribute this to Gandhi's teachings and influence (even though there were also other factors). Consequently, Gandhi is remembered around the world as a man of peace and moral courage in the fight against oppression and injustice.

WHAT IS THE SIGN OR SYMBOL "OM"? WHAT DOES IT MEAN?

The "om" or "aum" is a written symbol (page xvi) as well as a sound in Hinduism and other religions indigenous to India. Thus, it shows up frequently in art and writing, as well as in chanting or prayers during meditation. It represents the primal sound or the sound of the cosmos. When we chant it, we plug in to the sound or vibration of the cosmos. As a symbol, it points to our ability to become aligned with the deeper divine reality inside all existence. As a sound, it entices us to enter into that divine reality (or bring that reality into our consciousness) through our own voice and our own hearing of that sound.

How Hinduism Relates to Other Major Religions

Hinduism is deeply connected to other religions that developed in India, including Buddhism, Jainism, and Sikhism. This connection spans from the influence of Jainism's teaching of noninjury to Hindu attitudes toward vegetarianism (page 14) to many other facets of each faith.

- Hinduism is the "parent" religion to Buddhism, since Siddhartha Gautama (the Buddha's given name) was himself a Hindu, and incorporated key ideas from his native religion into what became Buddhism. These ideas include karma and reincarnation (page 7), and also the meditative model of spiritual practice whereby a person achieves enlightenment through training the mind via meditation.

- The daily reverence Sikhs pay to the *Adi Granth*, their sacred text, resembles some of the features of puja worship (page 11). For example, the text may be circled in flower garlands or set atop a decorated platform with candles on a home altar.

- Sikhs understand the divine to be more than just an individual deity; they view it as a cosmic divine force that permeates all existence, similar to the Hindu notion of Brahman.

- Islam and Hinduism, which have significantly different religious worldviews, have coexisted in India for extended periods of time. During the Mughal period in India, Muslims and Hindus lived peacefully together for many generations. Their respective theologians and religious leaders even studied together and challenged each other's ideas in a positive, engaging way.

- Despite long periods of harmony between Muslims and Hindus, conflict has occurred throughout the ages as well. For example, in 1947, as India gained independence from Britain, the British partitioned northern India along religious lines to create Pakistan. This resulted in a refugee crisis, upheaval, and violence.

THE STAR OF DAVID, PAGE 40

CHAPTER TWO

Judaism

Judaism is one of the oldest organized religions in the world; its history can be traced back about 3,500 years or more. At the heart of Judaism are two main concepts: monotheism and covenant. Monotheism refers to the belief in one god or deity. Covenant, according to Jewish teaching, refers to the relationship that exists between the deity—whom the Jewish people call "God"—and the adherents of the religion. Jewish scriptures tell of the special covenant relationship between God and his people throughout history, from the time of the ancient Israelites' enslavement in Egypt, through their wanderings in search of a promised homeland, their captivities by other nations, and beyond.

Judaism is a relatively small religion in terms of adherents; there are only around 15 million Jews in the world. A few factors contribute to the small number. First, 6 million Jews were killed in the Holocaust during World War II. Second, Judaism is one of the few major religions that is passed down by birth—a Jewish mother gives birth to a Jewish child. While it is possible to convert to Judaism, most Jewish people are born into the religion, and birth rates among Jewish people overall have been declining for the last several decades.

Despite its small numbers, however, Judaism is an enormously influential religion. Its root idea of monotheism has spread throughout the world as Jews themselves have lived nearly everywhere. Moreover, Judaism is the parent religion of the two largest religions in the world, Christianity and Islam, which account for over half the earth's human population.

Cheat Sheet

When it began: about 3,500 years ago

Number of adherents: about 15 million

Percentage of world population: 0.2 percent

Primary location: 80 percent of the world's Jews live in the United States (50 percent) or Israel (30 percent)

Largest sect/denomination: over a third of Jews worldwide practice Reform Judaism—though Orthodox Judaism, the smallest sect overall, has a strong presence

Primary text: *the Jewish Bible,* which includes the Torah, the Prophets, and the Writings (what Christians call the "Old Testament"); Jews will often use the term "Torah" to mean the entire Jewish Bible

Most recognizable symbol: the Star of David (page 22)

KEY DATES

C. 1750 BCE	The age of Abraham, the first of the patriarchs of ancient Israel mentioned in the Torah.
C. 1250 BCE	The age of Moses, the "lawgiver" who led the ancient Israelites out of slavery, according to the biblical narrative.
C. 1000 BCE	The "Golden Age" of Israel, including reigns of Kings Saul, David, and Solomon. The first temple is built in Jerusalem.
800 BCE–200 CE	Jewish biblical texts are written and canonized.
428 BCE	Second temple dedicated in Jerusalem after the first one was destroyed in 586 BCE by the Babylonians.
230 BCE–400 CE	Jewish homeland is under Roman rule.
70 CE	The Second Temple is destroyed by the Romans.
70–500	"Rabbinic" Judaism, oriented around synagogue and texts, is developed, as is the Talmud (a work of Jewish law and textual commentary on the Torah).
638	The Islamic conquest of Jerusalem.
1040	Birth of Rabbi Solomon ben Isaac, called Rashi—a medieval sage famous for his commentaries on the Talmud and the Jewish Bible.
1066–1480	Jews experience varying degrees of tolerance and persecution throughout Europe and the Middle East. Culminates in the Spanish Inquisition, in which many hundreds of Jews and others are killed, imprisoned, or exiled.
1700	Birth of Israel Baal Shem Tov, the founder of Hasidic Judaism.
1729	Birth of Moses Mendelssohn, a great Jewish enlightenment scholar.
1880s	Violent pogroms targeting Jews begin in Russia. Many relocate to Eastern Europe. Ottomans welcome Jews into their Empire.
1896	Theodor Herzl publishes *The Jewish State*, a major Zionist text calling for Jews to return to their traditional homeland.
1938–1945	Six million Jews, alongside other groups, are murdered while many others are imprisoned during the Holocaust—a mass genocide perpetrated by the Nazi Party during World War II.
1948	Modern-day Israel, a Jewish democratic state, is founded.

On the Jewish Calendar

PURIM

February or March

Sometimes also called the "Festival of Lots," Purim celebrates the biblical heroine Esther. Haman, an advisor to the king, planned to cast "lots" to pick a day to kill all the Jews in the kingdom; Esther and her cousin, Mordecai, instead convinced the king to spare the Jewish people. The holiday includes food and drink, wearing costumes, and giving to charity.

PESACH

March or April

Pesach, or "Passover," commemorates the biblical story of God's deliverance of the ancient Israelites from slavery in Egypt. It involves the *seder*, a special meal involving unleavened bread and other foods mentioned in the story.

SHAVUOT

May or June

Known as the "Feast of Weeks," Shavuot takes place 50 days after Pesach and celebrates the biblical story of the giving of the Torah on Mount Sinai. It coincides with grain harvests in traditional agricultural communities.

ROSH HASHANAH

September or October

Rosh Hashanah marks the New Year on the traditional Jewish calendar. Rather than simply marking one day, it is a 10-day period of self-reflection, ending on Yom Kippur.

YOM KIPPUR

September or October

Known as the "Day of Atonement," this is the holiest day on the Jewish calendar and a time of fasting, prayer, and repentance.

SUKKOT

September or October

Translated as "booths" or "tabernacles," Sukkot is a seven-day fall harvest holiday that commemorates the Israelites who wandered in the desert for 40 years after being freed from slavery. It is celebrated by erecting a booth or tent and eating in it for the week.

HANUKKAH

November or December

Hanukkah, also called the "Festival of Lights," commemorates a Jewish revolt against ancient Greek rulers. The story tells of an oil lamp owned by the Jewish rebels that only had enough oil to burn for one night but miraculously burned for eight nights. The menorah, which holds eight (or sometimes nine) candles, symbolizes this event.

Burning Questions

WHO STARTED JUDAISM?

Judaism has no single founder. It emerged as a formal entity—with clergy, ethical codes, laws, texts, and ritual observances—from the religion of the Israelites, or

Hebrew people, in the ancient Near East. Some scholars specifically distinguish between the religion of the Israelites and formal Judaism.

One of the differences between the two groups has to do with monotheism—the belief in one deity. The ancient Israelites seemed to revere their God as the highest, most supreme deity, but not necessarily as the *only* deity. Stories in the book of Genesis tell of the prophets of God competing with the prophets of Baal, a rival deity, to see which deity was the most powerful. Even in the famous Ten Commandments that Moses brought down from Mount Sinai (you've seen the movie, right?), God says for Israelites to "have no other gods before me" instead of saying "there are no other gods" or "all other gods are false." But as the ancient religion evolved, its monotheism became more established. That evolution took place through countless thinkers, historical contexts, texts, prolonged reflections, and more.

WHO WAS ABRAHAM, AND WHAT IS HIS ROLE IN JUDAISM?

Abraham is considered the first or primary patriarch in Judaism because God chose to form a covenant relationship with him and his descendants. The biblical phrase associated with him is "the father of many nations" for the promise that God made to him that his descendants would become the Jewish people who would live throughout the world. Most scholars place his lifetime somewhere between 1800 and 1700 BCE. He is known for his marriage to Sarah and for their son,

Isaac, who was born in their old age. Initially, Sarah feared she would not be able to conceive, so she gave her maidservant Hagar to Abraham, so he could fulfill his role as the father of many nations. The descendants of Hagar's son, Ishmael, are believed to be the founders and followers of Islam.

WHO WAS MOSES, AND WHAT IS HIS ROLE IN JUDAISM?

Moses is perhaps more famous than Abraham, due to the many popular movies that have been made about him and his role in delivering the Hebrew people from slavery in Egypt. The biblical story says that when Moses was an infant, the Egyptian pharaoh ordered the infant sons of all Hebrew women to be put to death in order to maintain population control over his slaves. To keep him safe, Moses' mother hid him in the reeds of the Nile River, where he was found by an Egyptian princess while she was bathing.

The Egyptian princess raised Moses in the palace as her own son; however, he saw the suffering of his people and, through a series of events, embarked upon a divine mission to convince Pharaoh to let the Hebrew people go free. As Pharaoh refused, Moses (with God's help) rained down plagues, fire, and other maladies onto the Egyptian people, culminating in the Angel of Death passing over Egypt and killing the firstborn of every Egyptian family.

Finally, Pharaoh relented and Moses led his people out of Egypt and into the wilderness to find the land God promised them as a homeland. During the journey, God revealed to Moses the laws, codes, and religious rituals that brought a great deal of structure to the religion of the ancient Israelites. For this reason, Moses is often called "the lawgiver" because through him, God reinstituted his covenant with his people and gave them rules for establishing their community.

WHAT IS THE TORAH? IS THAT THE JEWISH BIBLE?

The Torah is the first five books of the Jewish Bible: *Genesis, Exodus, Leviticus, Numbers,* and *Deuteronomy.* This is why this section is sometimes called the Pentateuch (meaning "five books"), though the word Torah is also sometimes used as a general term for all Jewish scriptures, not just the first five books.

The Torah contains the stories of creation and the first inhabitants of the world; of God's covenant with Abraham and his descendants (the patriarchs); of Moses and the dramatic deliverance from Egypt; of the Israelites' wanderings toward a homeland; and of the myriad codes, rules, rituals, and traditions that guide and establish life in the Jewish community.

The other two major sections of the Jewish Bible are called the Prophets and the Writings. The Prophets contains the books attributed to Isaiah, Jeremiah, Ezekiel, Amos, and many others. The Writings includes texts like Psalms, Proverbs, Song of Solomon, and a few others.

The Jewish Bible contains history, poetry, prose, religious instructions, prophecy, and more that was written, gathered, and formalized over a period of many hundreds of years. Some refer to the Jewish Bible with the term "Tanakh," which is a spoken anacronym (TNK) for the three main sections of the sacred text: Torah (the Pentateuch), Nevi'im (Prophetic books), and Ketuvim (the Writings).

IS THE JEWISH BIBLE THE SAME AS THE OLD TESTAMENT IN THE CHRISTIAN BIBLE?

The Jewish Bible is very similar to the Old Testament in many versions of the Christian Bible, albeit arranged differently. As Christianity emerged from Judaism, Christians continued to honor the Jewish sacred texts (Torah, Prophets, Writings) as sacred scripture and named them the Old Testament. They would add their own scriptures—the New Testament—to the Jewish text to create the Christian *Bible*. So, while Christians revere the Jewish scriptures, Jews continue to revere only the Jewish sacred texts.

I'VE ALSO HEARD OF THE TALMUD. WHAT IS THAT?

The Talmud is a large collection of interpretations, reflections, and discussions of the Torah and other parts of Jewish scripture by esteemed scholars and teachers. Some parts of it are so influential they are revered as an "oral Torah" alongside the written Torah in the Jewish Bible. The Talmud was first collected between 300 and 400 CE in two different versions: a Palestinian and a Babylonian. Over time, the work of medieval scholars like Rashi and Maimonides was added to the Talmud.

JEWISH MEN SOMETIMES WEAR LITTLE HATS, SHAWLS, AND LONG CURLS. IS THAT PART OF THE JEWISH LAW FOR DAILY LIVING?

Yes, sort of. The small, round hat or skullcap is called a yarmulke (or kippah), and many Jewish men will wear it during any religious occasion, like weddings, funerals, prayer services (including interfaith services), and so on. Some observant men wear yarmulkes all the time as a way of honoring God. Some Jewish women will also wear scarves as a head covering to honor God.

Some Jewish men pray while wearing phylacteries—small boxes that contain tiny pieces of Torah, attached to leather strings—to obey the biblical command that the people of God keep the divine law in their minds and hearts always. Men (especially Orthodox Jews) may use the strings to affix the little boxes to their left arm and forehead during prayers. Many Jewish men also pray with a prayer shawl draped over their shoulders.

Though yarmulkes and head coverings are used in many different sects, some distinctive forms of dress are common only in the Orthodox and ultra-Orthodox communities. In these communities, men may wear long hair or curls on either side of their faces, following a scriptural injunction that scholars have interpreted to mean that men should not cut or shave the sides of their heads. Other aspects of ultra-Orthodox dress—black coats or cloaks, fur hats—are not so much biblical as traditional. Here, observant Jewish people are doing what many believers do in other religions: dressing in a way that sets them apart from others reminds

Everyday Judaism

Keeping Kosher

Among Judaism's various exhortations for daily living are the kosher codes for eating. The term "kosher" comes from the Hebrew root that means "clean, pure, or proper." Kosher foods are those foods that Jewish dietary law deems to be proper to eat. Common foods that are *not* kosher include pork and shellfish; the practice of mixing meat with dairy (such as a beef burger with cheese or beef steak with cream gravy) is also not kosher.

Not all Jews adhere to the kosher codes, but those who do are careful to eat only those foods deemed by scripture, tradition, or current rabbinic authority as proper for Jews to eat. Moreover, some kosher Jewish households and restaurants maintain separate sets of dishes, cookware, and even refrigerators for meat and for dairy so that the two never mix in any way. Some scholars suggest that the kosher codes were developed because they served as health measures for a group of people who lived nomadic lives in a desert climate. Others suggest that the kosher codes are a way of bringing obedience to God's commands into one's everyday life.

themselves and others of their faith, and honors their faith through the mundane, everyday activity of wearing clothes.

JUDAISM SPEAKS OF A TEMPLE, BUT I'VE ALSO HEARD OF JEWS ATTENDING SYNAGOGUE. WHAT'S THE DIFFERENCE?

Temple and synagogue are the two main forms of sacred space in Judaism. The temple is the oldest form and can be traced back to the biblical period. The biblical story says that King David was given the plans for the temple in Jerusalem, but his son, King Solomon, actually had it built. Judaism at the time was a priestly religion, and Jewish worship was centered around sacrifice to God. People would bring animals or food to be offered to God in sacrifice for various reasons (forgiveness of sins, to make a request of God, etc.). The temple was destroyed by Babylonians in the 6th century BCE, and then it was later rebuilt.

When the Jewish people were taken into captivity in the 6th century BCE, they were forced away from their temple and had to adapt. Thus, an alternative form of sacred space and clergy slowly evolved: the synagogue and rabbis. Synagogue worship is not focused on sacrifices but instead is oriented around reading and understanding the texts, teachings, and traditions of Judaism, as well as keeping the high holidays. Rabbis are trained scholars and preachers who guide the congregation in their worship and practice.

The Second Temple was destroyed again by Romans in 70 CE, and has never been rebuilt. The only remnant of the temple, called the Western Wall, still stands in Israel and is a holy site for Jews (and Christians) all over the world. The Dome of the Rock mosque is also built on that site and is one of the holiest places in the world for Muslims.

Orthodox Jews look to a time in the future when the temple will be rebuilt on its historic site in Jerusalem and sacrifices to God will be restored. Synagogue worship, however, has been the dominant form of Jewish practice for over 2,000 years now.

The transition from temple worship to synagogue worship is a striking example of how religions change and adapt over time to stay relevant to the people who practice them.

YOU'VE MENTIONED ORTHODOX JEWS— IS THAT A CERTAIN GROUP IN JUDAISM?

Yes, Orthodox Jews (including ultra-Orthodox subdivisions) form one main group inside Judaism. Orthodox Jews practice the faith in the most traditional and historical ways that trace back for centuries. They are most likely to wear distinctive dress, maintain traditional gender roles at home and in worship, keep strict kosher observances, and adhere to other Jewish laws. There are different branches within Orthodox Judaism that have their own distinct histories, leaders, and traditions.

WHAT ARE THE OTHER GROUPS INSIDE JUDAISM?

The three primary groups within Judaism are Orthodox, Reform, and Conservative. Reform Judaism developed in the 19th century as a modernist innovation that reflects scientific enlightenment thinking. It is the most dominant form of Judaism worldwide, especially outside of Israel. Reform Jews focus on the ethical aspects of their faith rather than on keeping strict observances of the Jewish law. They may or may not keep kosher, participate in all the religious holidays, or marry within the faith.

Conservative Judaism was developed in the 19th century, not long after Reform Judaism, in order to offer a "midpoint" between Reform and Orthodox. Its leaders felt that Reform Judaism left too much of the Jewish tradition behind. Conservative Jews keep some of the traditions and laws of Judaism deemed most important. They may also keep kosher and make room for messianic expectation, which is common among many Orthodox Jews. There are other groups inside Judaism (i.e., Reconstructionist, Zionist), but Orthodox, Reform, and Conservative are the main ones to which the vast majority of Jews belong.

ARE JEWS WAITING FOR A MESSIAH?

Yes and no. The Jewish biblical texts speak of a messiah or savior figure who will come to rescue the Jewish people from persecutions, exile, and other suffering. The biblical tradition of messiah expanded and continued among some Jewish groups through history and is retained in some groups today. Some groups inside Judaism think of the messiah not so much as a person but as an age or era of time. The messianic age, in this view, will come at some point in the future and bring with it the restoration of the unified Jewish community. Still others say that the messiah already came or the messianic age began when the state of Israel was established in 1948; according to the latter view, the founding of Israel set the context for the Jewish people scattered throughout the world to return to their homeland and live together in community as God's people. Finally, many Jews—especially Reform Jews—don't hold to any sort of belief in a coming messiah or messianic age.

WHAT DOES JUDAISM SAY ABOUT THE AFTERLIFE?

Judaism does not place much emphasis on the afterlife, which may seem surprising since Christianity and Islam, the two religions that emerged from Judaism, put a heavy focus on the afterlife.

Jewish tradition will speak of Abraham's bosom as a place of rest for people who have passed away. Another biblical reference is to Sheol, a place of darkness where the dead go—sort of like Hades for the Greeks. Some Jewish groups believe in the resurrection of the body at the end of times or when the messiah comes, which is connected to some sort of afterlife belief. At any rate, Judaism does not have a uniform teaching on the afterlife, mainly because its central focus is on this life. All the laws, commandments, and traditions in Judaism revolve around human action *in this life* and the benefit *in this life* that accrues from that action. Thus, Judaism is often referred to as a "this-worldly" religion, as opposed to an "otherworldly" religion.

WHICH HOLIDAYS ARE MOST IMPORTANT FOR PRACTICING JEWS?

Some Jews (especially Orthodox and Conservative) will observe nearly all the holidays on the Jewish calendar (see "On the Jewish Calendar," page 26). The holidays most important to the vast majority of Jews, however, are Yom Kippur, Passover, and the weekly Sabbath, or Shabbat.

WHY DO PEOPLE BURN CANDLES IN MENORAHS AT HANUKKAH?

The menorah—a candelabra with holders for eight or nine candles— has become a common symbol of Judaism alongside the Star of David. The menorah is part of Hanukkah, a holiday that occurs in December to commemorate a Jewish revolt against Roman rule. The story of the revolt tells of an oil lamp that only had enough oil for one night but miraculously didn't run out of oil for eight days. So, the eight candles on the menorah symbolize those eight days of revolt and the miracle that occurred. The ninth candle placed in the middle of some menorahs is simply the "lighting" candle used to light the other ones, one at a time, for each of the eight days of celebration.

Everyday Judaism

Observing the Sabbath

A regular part of Jewish life is the weekly holy day called the Sabbath, or *Shabbat*. The Sabbath occurs on the seventh day of each week, which begins on Friday night at sundown and ends Saturday night at sundown. The Sabbath tradition comes from the biblical account in *Genesis* of God's creation of the earth in six days and his resting on the seventh day. Additionally, the biblical text lists "keeping the Sabbath holy" as one of the Ten Commandments that Moses received from God on Mount Sinai. Meal preparation is done beforehand so that little to no work has to be done on the Sabbath. In Israel, as well as in some predominantly Jewish neighborhoods and business districts outside of Israel, shops close, public transportation shuts down, and generally all public activity ceases during the Sabbath. Jewish families usually celebrate the Sabbath together in their homes by eating a meal together, reading and discussing the Torah, and—most importantly—resting.

WHAT IS THE STAR OF DAVID?

The Star of David—also called the Shield of David—is a six-pointed star made from two triangles superimposed on each other. The symbol was used sporadically by Jewish communities beginning in the 1700s, but it became more universally used by Jewish groups and others when it was adopted in the 19th century by Zionism. In the 20th century, the Star of David was the symbol Jews were forced to wear under Nazism and during the Holocaust. Today, the symbol is the most common symbol of Judaism across cultures, making it analogous to the cross for Christians or the crescent for Muslims.

WHAT IS A BAR MITZVAH?

A bar mitzvah—a term that literally means "son of the commandments"—is a ceremony that honors a young man's 13th birthday, an age that symbolizes leaving childhood and moving into manhood. The ceremony, wherein the young man reads from the Jewish Bible in front of friends and family, marks his coming of age; the young man will now be held accountable for his actions under Jewish law and is allowed (even expected) to participate in full adult worship. Traditionally, this ritual was for males only; however, starting in the early 20th century, girls at the age of 12 or 13 have been allowed to have a bat mitzvah, wherein they become daughters of the commandments, with similar rights and responsibilities with regard to Jewish law, custom, and religious practice.

WHERE HAVE JEWS LIVED HISTORICALLY?

While the ancestral homeland of the Jewish people lies in modern-day Israel, Jewish population centers have shifted greatly over the millennia, largely due to persecution and expulsions, beginning with Assyrian exile around 740 BCE. Prior to the 20th century, there were large migrations of Jewish communities throughout the Middle East, Northern Africa, Europe, and beyond. As minorities in each new land they settled in, Jewish people faced varying forms of prejudice, known as anti-Semitism, which continued the cycle of exile and resettlement.

Despite this, there have been many periods of peaceful coexistence with the predominant faiths of the regions where Jews settled. During the Spanish Inquisition, when Jews and heretical Christians were being burned at the stake, the Ottomans (a Turkish Muslim empire) welcomed them. Prior to that period in Spain, during the Moorish period (a Muslim empire), people from all three religions lived together peacefully and were part of a renaissance of learning in science, mathematics, and the arts. While there have been religious and political conflicts among these groups throughout the centuries, there is nothing in Judaism, Christianity, or Islam that opposes the peaceful coexistence of the faithful of these religions.

HOW DID THE HOLOCAUST IMPACT JUDAISM?

During the Holocaust of World War II, between 1941 and 1945, about 6 million Jews were systematically killed by Nazi Germany and its collaborators. The event is called the Shoah in Judaism, meaning "catastrophe" in

Hebrew. The impact of this period on Judaism and the Jewish people cannot be overstated. The "Final Solution" perpetrated under Adolf Hitler was perhaps the worst persecution to ever be directed at the Jewish people as a whole. What made it particularly horrific is that it happened at the hands of what was lauded at the time as the most technologically and scientifically advanced country in Western civilization. Instead of using that progress to benefit humanity, Germany used its technological prowess to round up, transport, and kill many millions of Jews—as well as Romani peoples (then called gypsies), homosexuals, Jehovah's Witnesses, political dissidents, and others—in concentration camps.

After the liberation of the camps by the Allied powers, many Jewish people who survived immigrated to the United States or to the newly formed state of Israel. Indeed, the horrors of the Holocaust was a major factor in the Allied powers having the political will to establish a formal homeland for the Jews. Theologically, many Jewish scholars struggled with how God could allow his covenant people to undergo such a horrible genocide. Some Jews emerged as atheists, saying God is dead or at least the covenant between God and the Jews is finished. Others reflected deeply and came to different conclusions. Regardless, world Judaism was altered irrevocably. The slogan "Never again" has come to mean that such a genocide should never happen again to Jews or any other people. Sadly, the anti-Semitism that spawned the Holocaust still exists. Jews worldwide still suffer on a regular basis from anti-Semitic attacks on their synagogues, cemeteries, and businesses.

WHAT IS THE IMPORTANCE OF ISRAEL
TO THE JEWISH PEOPLE?

The geographic area known today as Israel is an area
referred to in the Jewish biblical texts as "the promised
land" or "the land flowing with milk and honey." It is the
place that God promised to his people after he delivered
them from slavery in Egypt. Many sections of the biblical
texts tell of the conflicts the ancient Hebrew people had
with the other inhabitants of the land as they struggled to
claim the area they believed God had given to them. The
First and Second Temples were built in Jerusalem, and
the land now called Israel was, for a time, governed by the
Jewish people themselves. As that geographic area was
taken over by many different empires over the centuries,
the Jewish people either stayed in the land under foreign
rule, were cast out, or left of their own accord.

Centuries of persecution around the world led many
Jews to embrace Zionism, the idea that they could
secure their safety best if they had their own homeland again, as they did in the time of Kings David and
Solomon. By the end of the 19th century, many Jews
throughout the world started to move back to what had
been their homeland. After the Holocaust, the Allied
powers gathered the political will to create the modern
state of Israel as a homeland for the Jewish people. The
Palestinian people, who also have lived in that same
geographic region for thousands of years, were to have
their own state in the area as well. But the Palestinian
state has yet to be created.

How Judaism Relates to Other Major Religions

Judaism is the oldest monotheistic world religion, and it is the "parent" religion to the two largest religions in the world: Christianity and Islam. As a result, there are many resonances among these three religions, even though their differences are stark.

- While Judaism, Christianity, and Islam revere the same God as the one true God, their respective understandings of that God and his dealings with humanity vary significantly. That said, there are core ideas that run through all three religions, including the belief that God is a personal deity, not an impersonal force or reality like Brahman in Hinduism or the Tao in Taoism; the idea that God intervenes in the world and interacts with specific individuals and groups of people throughout history; the idea that a relationship with God is vital for life's meaning and human thriving; the idea that obedience and submission to God restores relationship with God and creates the possibility of blessedness here on earth and (for Christians and Muslims) in the afterlife.

- Although Jesus himself was Jewish, Christianity came to extol Jesus as divine, which marks a sharp divergence from Judaism. Christianity preserves its monotheism by seeing Jesus as the "son" of God— one of the three "personages" of the one God. Judaism rejects this notion (as does Islam). For Judaism, monotheism means simply what it says: There is one God, and God does not have a "son."

- Many adherents of Christianity and Islam claim that they worship the same God as the God of the Jews. Many Jews might agree, but some may be hesitant to affirm this simply because Christians and Muslims present God in such radically different ways than the Jewish traditions present God. For instance, the Christian doctrine of the Trinity is foreign to Judaism.

- For Islam, Muhammad is the last and final prophet in a long line of prophets that stretches back to Abraham and, even before that, to Adam and Noah. Judaism doesn't generally view Adam or Noah as prophets, nor does it revere Muhammad as having equal standing in the Jewish prophetic lineage. In short, Jews don't think that God had called Muhammad to be a prophet.

THE YIN AND YANG SYMBOL, PAGE 64

CHAPTER THREE

Taoism

Taoism is one of the indigenous religions of China and has existed in a distinct religious form for about 2,200 years. Taoism, like Confucianism (another Chinese indigenous religion) and Buddhism (which came to China from India), blends with ancient popular religious traditions in China that predate it. Among these ancient traditions are ancestor worship, shamanistic practices designed to mediate between the world of spirits and the human world, and various practices intended to optimize the body for spiritual achievement.

Taoism brings to these traditions an increased focus on achieving harmony in life and with nature and on perfecting the spiritual disciplines and rituals required to achieve personal transformation for oneself and one's deceased ancestors. This personal transformation could include longevity accompanied by a healthy body and mind and even achieving spiritual immortality, whereby one escapes the limitations of the physical body and becomes "eternal" or one of the "immortal ones."

Taoism is distinct from other religions in that it has neither a rigid organizational structure, nor holy sites like Mecca or Jerusalem, nor a leader like the Pope or Dalai Lama. In fact, many who practice Taoist rituals and activities do not even self-identify as Taoist. However, it wields significant influence on the history, beliefs, and traditions in China—the world's most populous nation—and beyond. It is an integral part of the long-established, popular religious culture of China, influencing nearly all aspects of daily life while offering paths of esoteric spiritual achievement that require extraordinary discipline and focus for its most devout followers.

Cheat Sheet

When it began: between the 3rd and 2nd centuries BCE, although tradition holds that its founder, Lao tzu, lived in the 6th century BCE

Number of adherents: 100 million regularly participate in Taoist ritual or activity, although as few as 8 million self-identify as Taoist

Percentage of world population: less than 1 percent self-identify as Taoist, although its influence extends much further

Primary location: China and anywhere Chinese culture has spread, most prominently in Japan

Largest sect/denomination: in religious Taoism, the Celestial Masters school and the Perfect Realization school; philosophical Taoism isn't really divided into groups or schools

Primary text: the *Tao Te Ching*, the *Chuang tzu*, the *Three Caverns* (which includes the first two, plus over 1,400 additional texts)

Most recognizable symbol: yin and yang (page 46)

KEY DATES

6th CENTURY BCE	Lao tzu, founder of Taoism, lives.
4th CENTURY BCE	Influential Taoist master Chuang tzu lives.
3rd CENTURY BCE–2nd CENTURY CE	The texts of *Tao Te Ching* and the *Chuang tzu* are compiled—these are the heart of philosophical Taoism.
202 BCE–221CE	Han Dynasty, during which religious Taoism emerged as a distinct set of rituals, beliefs, teachings, and texts.
34–156 CE	Zhang Dao Ling, who began the "Five Bushels of Rice" movement, which became the Celestial Masters school of thought in religious Taoism, lives.
3rd–4th CENTURIES	Development of several schools in Neo-Taoism, including the Secret Mystical Teaching school and the Pure Conversation school.
618–906	Tang dynasty, under which Taoism flourished and developed after a period of minimal imperial support.
1000–1250	Several attempts are made to create a collected Taoist canon that would include all the sacred texts of Taoism.
1260–1368	Yuan dynasty, under which Taoist monasteries and libraries were destroyed.
1444	Publication of *the Dao Zhang*, the definitive anthology of Taoist sacred texts. It includes the works of Lao tzu and Chuang tzu, as well as over 5,000 scroll volumes of more than 1,400 additional works of Taoist religion. It is also called the *Three Caverns*, after the names of its three main sections.
1368–1644	Ming dynasty, under which Taoism enjoys imperial support and Taoist leaders gain official positions.
1644–1911	Qing (or Manchu) dynasty, under which Taoism struggles for support.
1911–PRESENT	Taoism and other official religions recognized by the Chinese government survive (and even thrive, in some cases), except during the Cultural Revolution from 1966 to 1976, when any religious practice was forbidden.

On the Taoist Calendar

Many Taoist holidays are not exclusive to Taoism but are also celebrated by practitioners of other religions as well as by secularists. Accordingly, most prominent Taoist holidays are also general Chinese holidays.

CHINESE NEW YEAR

January or February

Families do deep cleaning to prepare for spring, perform worship to ancestors and gods, and celebrate with fireworks and gifts. Paper statues of gods may be burned so that the ashes fly up to the heavens to give a report on the humans below.

LANTERN FESTIVAL

February or March

This festival celebrates the birthday of Tianguan, a god of good fortune, during the first full moon of the year. People eat sweet dumplings, carry lanterns around in the streets, and release red lanterns into the air.

TOMB SWEEPING DAY

April

Also called "Pure Brightness" or the "Clear and Bright" festival, this event is focused on devotion to the ancestors. Families clean the tomb areas of relatives, picnic at the burial sites, and offer food to their deceased ancestors.

DRAGON BOAT FESTIVAL

June or July

People race boats decorated as dragons and eat special rice cakes. Taoist priests perform rituals to ward off evil spirits.

HUNGRY GHOST FESTIVAL

August or September

This is a Buddhist festival that Taoists and others celebrate, during which people set out food and drink to appease, calm, and revere the agitated, wandering ghosts of ancestors who did not receive a proper burial.

XIAYUAN FESTIVAL

November or December

This, the last of several annual Chinese Moon festivals, occurs during the 10th lunar month, just before the Chinese New Year. It is focused on reverence and worship of ancestors and other deities. Special paper clothes and pretend money are burned as offerings; food and drink are offered as well. Families eat together and prepare for the new year.

Burning Questions

WHO STARTED TAOISM?

The tradition holds that a sage named Lao tzu, who lived in China in the 6th century BCE, started Taoism. Not much is known about him, which leads some scholars to wonder if he actually existed; however, most view him as an actual historical figure. Lao tzu lived at the same time as Confucius, another great Chinese sage. According to one Taoist story, Confucius visited Lao tzu to ask his advice about life. Lao tzu reportedly told Confucius to quit his job and abandon his way of living for something more natural.

In another famous story, Lao tzu decides to leave China because of disillusionment with the country and its governors. He rode on a water buffalo to the border and a guard recognized him as a wise sage. The guard begged him not to leave China, but Lao tzu insisted. Finally, the guard convinced him to stay long enough to write down his wisdom to leave behind for future generations. Lao tzu lingered, wrote a small amount, handed it to the guard, and then left China forever. That book is now known as the *Tao Te Ching*, and the image of Lao tzu riding a water buffalo is a popular image of him throughout Asian art. Lao tzu and a later figure named Chuang tzu are the most important figures for philosophical Taoism (one main form of Taoism). The suffix "tzu" means "master" or "teacher."

WHO WAS CHUANG TZU?

Chuang tzu was a Taoist master who lived in northern China in the 4th century. He is credited with writing the second most important text in Taoism after the *Tao Te Ching*, a longer text called the *Chuang tzu*. The *Chuang tzu* contains stories, parables, and longer teachings that Chuang tzu himself might have written, but which were most likely written by his students and followers. Not much is known about him, but a fairly consistent portrait emerges from the text that carries his name. He was an unconventional person who gave little thought to social status, reputation, or appearances. Chuang tzu was critical of the Confucian approach to life through ritual and etiquette, as well as its constant extolling of the "ancient masters" as ideal role models. He was intelligent, clever, and possessed a biting wit. He confronted and even mocked leading thinkers and practitioners of Chinese philosophy. The "Old Master," Lao tzu, was the only ancient sage he revered. However, unlike Lao tzu, he had no interest in human society, governance, or politics. Instead, Chuang tzu preferred a life "off the beaten path" of civilization, a more solitary and individual life that resembled an "uncarved block" rather than the stylized life of someone shaped by the controlling influences of social conditioning.

HOW DOES TAOISM GET ITS NAME?

Taoism is named for the "Tao," which is an ancient and common concept found throughout Chinese religious culture, not just in Taoism. Tao is difficult to translate into English, but most scholars translate it as "the way" or "the path" and apply it to all of life and the cosmos. In other words, the Tao is the way of all things. It is the deep force of life and being in all of reality. Everything that exists is rooted in it; nothing exists outside of it. It is both imminent and transcendent, both subtle and obvious, like an invisible energy that flows through all of existence.

For Taoists and others in Chinese religion, the Tao is the "Supreme Ultimate." However, the Tao is a force, presence, or reality, not so much a god or personal deity. Human language can't even really capture or describe it properly. The Tao must be experienced, felt, intuited, or sensed. It is a mystical reality that cannot be reduced to logical analysis.

DOES TAOISM WORSHIP A GOD OR GODS AT ALL?

Yes and no. Many Taoists revere the Tao as a deep force or presence in all of nature and reality but do not relate to it as a personal god that one would pray to or perform rituals for. Other Taoists—specifically, religious Taoists—very much revere their ancestors as gods and erect shrines that they maintain to honor them in regular rituals. Ancestor worship and reverence has a long history in Chinese religion—and an even longer history than either Taoism or Confucianism—and both of those religions incorporate it into their respective beliefs and practices.

Religious Taoism specifically also reveres or worships important sages and spiritual leaders who have become deified, because people believe that they achieved immortality through their spiritual practice. Taoist shrines and temples feature statues and images of these gods or deified sages, and practitioners make offerings and prayers to them.

WHO ARE THE MAIN GODS IN RELIGIOUS TAOISM?

The most commonly worshipped gods are deified mortals—either historical figures or figures from legend who achieved immortality. These include the Jade Emperor, the highest god who is seen as an emanation of the Tao; the Yellow Emperor, who lived in the 3rd century BCE and was one of several ancient sages revered throughout Chinese religion; the Military Emperor, a 3rd-century military man named Guan Di (or Guan Gong) who was executed and is seen in his deified form as a guardian of the empire; and a group of deities called the Immortals, eight figures from both history and legend, each with distinct accoutrements, traits, and powers. All of these gods (and many others) have traditional, recognizable ways in which they are represented artistically in temples and shrines.

WHAT SCRIPTURES DOES TAOISM USE?

As mentioned earlier, two sacred foundational texts of Taoism are the *Tao Te Ching* and the *Chuang tzu*—credited to Lao tzu and Chuang tzu, respectively. In all likelihood, these texts were written or compiled by later disciples of these two men. The ultimate canon or standard primary texts of Taoism, however, is called the *Dao Zhang:* an anthology that includes the *Tao Te Ching*, the *Chuang tzu*, and over 1,400 other works produced by Taoist sages and masters up through the 13th century. This anthology is also sometimes called the *Three Caverns*, because its three main sections are named after caves or caverns.

Everyday Taoism

Temple Worship

China is filled with temples of varying sizes and degrees of ornateness. These temples often include a combination of Taoist and Buddhist imagery and practices. The proliferation of temples makes it easy for regular temple worship to be a common part of life for everyday practitioners of Chinese religion, including Taoists.

At its most basic, temple worship involves making offerings to one or more of the deities or immortal ones enshrined in the temple. The simplest offering is incense. Most temples have sticks of incense that worshippers can purchase to then light and take in as an offering to one of the gods. The worshipper could hold the incense stick in both hands in a prayerful pose, bow to the statue or image of the god, then offer the burning incense by standing it up in a nearby bowl of sand so that the aroma wafts around the god.

Other offerings may include food, drink, flowers, candy, or money. Some temples have pretend money made of gold paper to symbolize something permanent, valuable, and indestructible. Offering this to the god may symbolize the worshipper's devotion as permanent and indestructible and that their devotion and worship of the god is the most valuable thing in their life.

ARE PHILOSOPHICAL AND RELIGIOUS TAOISM THE MAJOR GROUPS OR SECTS AMONG TAOISTS?

Most scholars view Taoism as being practiced in these two basic ways, which tend to be very different from each other. Philosophical Taoists focus on the teachings of Lao tzu and Chuang tzu. Their teachings emphasize living a simple life rooted in the energy of the Tao revealed in nature. This form of Taoism often resembles nature mysticism and is more a way of life and worldview than a specific set of ritual practices. Religious, or "magical," Taoists root themselves in Lao tzu's teachings and blend in many traditions from shamanism and rituals common in Chinese religion. Many of these rituals are centered on funeral practices, proper respect for the dead, and achieving long life, vitality, and even immortality for oneself and one's ancestors. This form of Taoism more closely resembles what most people think of as a religion, with priests, rituals, and sacred spaces. In contrast, philosophical Taoism is more of a lifestyle, worldview, or philosophy (as its description suggests).

SO, IS TAOISM A RELIGION OR A PHILOSOPHY?

It's both. The nature mysticism of philosophical Taoism often results in people trying to live as simply and as naturally as possible, usually "off the beaten path" of whatever the current culture affirms. People inside religious Taoism, on the other hand, are more focused on rituals and other observances designed to honor ancestors and worship gods or others who have achieved immortality. This type of Taoism is oriented around a calendar of holidays and festival observances, many of which are scheduled according to moon cycles and other natural seasons. So, while these two forms of Taoism are very different in important ways, they are both rooted in a common worldview that situates our lives into a larger reality called the Tao.

WHAT KIND OF SACRED SPACE DOES TAOISM HAVE?

Taoism has several important sacred spaces. For philosophical Taoism, any space in proximity to striking aspects of the natural world is sacred. Specifically, Taoism recognizes several mountains as sacred, which is also a feature of Chinese religion as a whole. Rivers, streams, meadows, groves, and valleys can also serve as sacred spaces for Taoists. Religious Taoism erects temples of all sizes—some permanent, some temporary or mobile—in which priests and other clergy perform various rituals and observances. Finally, a more modest version of anything you might find in a temple may also be found in a home altar or shrine. Statues and images of deities or immortal ancestors, trays for offerings of food and drink or money, incense and incense holders, and so on; all of these are common items in both large temples and home altars.

WHAT ARE THE WAYS PEOPLE PRACTICE RELIGIOUS TAOISM?

The most common way is through regular temple worship (see "Everyday Taoism: Temple Worship" on page 56). Other ways include worshipping or honoring ancestors in a home altar or shrine, celebrating the major holidays (especially those that involve the ancestors), and participating in disciplines designed to bring immortality or at least longevity of life. These would include any number of movement, meditation, and breathing disciplines, as well as practices in alchemy.

WHAT IS ALCHEMY IN RELIGIOUS TAOISM?

In Taoism, alchemy refers to the use of elixirs to bring about beneficial energy shifts in the body with the goal of achieving longevity or immortality. Taoism speaks of the "outer elixir" (*wai-tan*) and the "inner elixir" (*nei-tan*). Outer elixirs involve many formulations or recipes of ingredients, such as cinnabar, jade, gold, and other substances, to create medicines or dietary supplements intended to properly balance or activate the body's vital energies. Inner elixirs include movement arts (like *qi gong, tai chi*, etc.), breathing techniques, and meditative practices.

WHAT TYPE OF CLERGY OR SPIRITUAL LEADERS DOES TAOISM HAVE?

Religious Taoism doesn't have a centralized religious authority or clerical hierarchy. Each different school of thought or tradition has its own ways of determining its leaders and their roles. That said, there are a few titles or roles that occur frequently across the different schools of thought inside religious Taoism. Priests usually live in monasteries and are called "masters of the Tao" (*dao shi*). They lead people in prayer or perform

Everyday Taoism

The Art of Qi Gong

Movement practices such as *qi gong* are some of the most popular ways in which Taoist practitioners attempt to achieve harmony, longevity, and perhaps even immortality in their lives. The term "qi" is usually translated as "energy," and "gong" is translated as "work," "effort," or "practice." So, a person who does qi gong is doing "energy work" or "energy practice."

Qi gong is a collection of physical movements and postures designed to distribute and manage the flow of energy, or qi, throughout the body. When someone's qi is blocked or stagnant, they may become ill, or they may struggle to achieve spiritual enlightenment of any kind. They may also be overcome with stress, anger, jealousy, fear, or other maladies of the mind or soul. Qi gong, through its slow, sweeping movements accompanied by specific meditations, visualizations, and disciplined breathing techniques, helps bring practitioners into harmony within themselves and with the natural world around them. Often, practitioners will do qi gong in the mornings at sunrise, when things are still peaceful and quiet, outside in a park, or in a place with a beautiful natural view.

rituals in temples, but like monks in other traditions, they are usually more focused on their own spiritual path. So, they teach others who live near lay leaders or "lay masters" (*shi gong*), who perform the array of rituals and observances that are required by the calendar or requested by worshippers. Sometimes these lay leaders have specialties that they become known for in their communities, such as healing or exorcism, and fulfill the same role that shamans do in other religions.

Lay masters who have been trained by priests from the dominant, more official schools of Taoism are called Black Hats (and wear, as the name suggests, a small black hat with a gold knot on the top). Black Hats are authorized to perform all the major rituals that accompany the major holidays and feast days. Another group of leaders, called the Red Hats, are not authorized by the monastic priests of the major schools to perform the most important rituals; however, they are sought out for exorcisms and other shamanic rituals that the Black Hats sometimes forgo in favor of the more prestigious observances.

IN WHAT WAYS DO SOME TAOIST PRIESTS FUNCTION LIKE SHAMANS?

A shaman is a person who serves as a mediator for whatever is considered divine—the spirit world, or the realm of the gods, however it might be conceived. Shamans often go into altered states of consciousness, such as trances, in order to deliver messages from the spirit world. Or they may temporarily "take on," or become consumed by, the personality of the deity or spirit they are mediating. Shamanism is a longstanding part of Chinese folk religion and has blended into the practices of religious Taoism. Taoist priests may serve as mediators between people and their deified ancestors or other spirits or gods with whom people wish to communicate.

WHAT ARE THE MAJOR SCHOOLS OR TRADITIONS WITHIN RELIGIOUS TAOISM?

The Celestial Masters school, founded in the mid-2nd century, is the oldest and most influential branch in religious Taoism. This school, more than any other, set the standards for Taoist rituals and how priests should observe them. The Perfect Realization school, founded in the 12th century, is the most prominent monastic community in Taoism and has several branches within it. The most influential branch today, the Lung Men branch, operates out of the White Cloud Monastery in Beijing. There are other schools that have had prominence in Taoism over the centuries but are not active today, including Great Oneness, Great Purity, Heavenly Mind, and others.

WHAT'S THE MOST IMPORTANT TEACHING IN PHILOSOPHICAL TAOISM, SINCE THEY DON'T REALLY FOCUS ON RITUALS OR TEMPLE OBSERVANCES?

Naturalness (*ziran*) and nonaction (*wu-wei*) are the two most touted virtues for philosophical Taoists. The basic Taoist view is that human beings are good and are designed to live alongside all other beings and entities in nature. However, when we try to control nature or bend others to our will, things get out of balance, which can cause disruptive, bad, and even evil things to occur. Taoism also teaches that everything and everyone thrives and is happy when they are doing what is "natural" to them—whatever it is they are designed to do and be. A tree, for example, is designed to grow into the shape, size, and colors its inherent properties deem it "natural" to grow into. To try to force it to grow differently—into a smaller or larger size, to have a different kind of leaf or bark, or to have a different color—would be to go against its nature. Both the tree and the person trying to force the tree to be something it's not designed to be would struggle in the process. The better path is to let the tree be what it is. There is no struggle when we do and are what we are naturally designed to do and be.

Nonaction relates directly to this. The tree doesn't have to do anything to become what it's naturally designed to become. There is no contrived, calculated action it has to undertake. Assuming it is planted in a hospitable environment, it simply has to stand there. No further action is needed. Naturalness and nonaction work together to create an easy flow of life for all things and people. This flow is the essential nature of the Tao. When we are living naturally, according to our deepest most authentic instincts, the actions we take and the effort we expend don't occur as a struggle or as work.

YOU'VE SAID THE IDEA OF THE "FLOW" OR THE "WAY" OF ALL THINGS IS IMPORTANT IN TAOISM. HOW DOES TAOISM EXPLAIN THIS?

The Tao is the way of all things, the natural flow of all existence. It is easy to accomplish because it exists at the most basic level of all things. Problems arise when we try to dominate, control, or manipulate ourselves, others, or the natural world into being or doing something it's not designed to be or do. We can experience ease, grace, and peace in our lives if we harmonize ourselves with the Tao. Usually, the way of all things involves an interplay of opposites that naturally balance each other over time. Life and death, joy and sadness, light and darkness, male and female, up and down, youth and old age, and so on. This natural interplay of opposites is symbolized in the circle of yin and yang (page 46). It is arguably the most common symbol in all of Chinese religion.

SO, THAT'S WHAT YIN AND YANG ARE—POLAR OPPOSITES?

Yes, yin is the dark and yang is the light portion of the symbol. The design of the circular symbol evokes a sense of endless flow—a constant movement back and forth between the two poles of opposing aspects of life. All of life flows in this interdependent, mutually affirming way. Taoism teaches that this interplay of opposites is completely natural and a part of the Tao. The more we accept it and harmonize our way of living and thinking to it, the more peaceful and joyful our lives can be.

IS HARMONY THE GOAL OF TAOISM?

Yes, in a nutshell. Harmony is the goal of all Chinese religion, but Taoism has its own ideas and teachings regarding how to attain it. Philosophical Taoists desire harmony within oneself, with others, with nature, and with the Tao. Religious Taoists desire this harmony, too, and seek to achieve it through ritual observance and proper worship of the ancestors and gods. Immortality has also come to be an ultimate goal for religious Taoists.

YOU MENTIONED THAT TAOISM AND CONFUCIANISM HAVE A SHARED HISTORY. HOW DO THEIR BELIEFS DIFFER?

The early Taoist master Lao tzu lived at the same time as Confucius, in the 6th century BCE (see page 52). Confucius was a philosopher and government official whose philosophy focused on achieving harmony in society via adherence to the rules of etiquette that applied to every aspect of life, both public and private. Confucian scholars were highly learned men who spent years studying and perfecting the teachings of the Confucian classical texts and traditions; they were highly cultivated individuals who knew well the intricacies of etiquette and ritual for every possible situation.

Taoism, arising alongside Confucianism, took a very different approach to achieving harmony in life and society—an approach that was often harshly critical of the Confucian path. For Taoists like Chuang tzu and others, submitting oneself to the rigors of Confucian study and behavioral etiquette for years on end was the most unnatural way to live. Moreover, far from creating harmony in the individual or society, Taoists argued that such strict behavioral rules would damage people's natural instincts for being human. Many episodes in Taoist literature detail the arguments between famous Taoist sages and Confucian scholars. Despite their significant differences, both traditions are rooted in the same aspects of Chinese folk religion that predate them. Some scholars suggest that Confucianism and Taoism are the yin and yang of Chinese religion—polar opposites that exist interdependently with each other in a natural flow of give and take.

WHERE IS TAOISM PRACTICED BEYOND MAINLAND CHINA?

Taoism is popular in places beyond mainland China, including Hong Kong, Taiwan, and Singapore. In the United States, religious Taoism has been practiced for many generations among Chinese communities, particularly in major cities such as San Francisco. Most people outside of Chinese heritage who practice Taoism, however, have adopted its philosophical form, not its religious form. Taoist philosophy, especially as it is expressed in the *Tao Te Ching*, is popular in many parts of the world, including the West.

How Taoism Relates to Other Major Religions

There's a popular saying that captures the complexity of Chinese religion as a whole: "In China, everyone wears a Confucian cap, a Taoist robe, and Buddhist sandals." This saying points to a truth about Chinese religion that can be confusing to outsiders—namely, that the traditions of three distinct religions blend together in Chinese religion in ways that make perfect sense to those who practice them.

- Like Confucianism and Buddhism, Taoism focuses more on proper practice than on proper adherence to creeds or doctrines. Such religions tend to allow a great deal of diversity of ideas not only within themselves but also with other religions. For this reason, the three faiths have blended together in rich and complex ways for thousands of years in China. For example, a Taoist temple may include statues of a Buddhist bodhisattva, and a Taoist priest may use Buddhist meditation techniques in spiritual practice.

- Taoism and Confucianism are rooted in the Chinese folk religion that predates them. Taoism focuses primarily on nature, while Confucianism is focused on improving society.

Continued >

- When Japan imported Chinese culture during the Heian period (between the 8th and 12th centuries), a fourth religion was added to the blend of Chinese religion: Shinto, the indigenous religion of Japan.

- The Tao bears similarity to the Hindu concept of Brahman. Both are impersonal forces that are revered as the highest, most ultimate, and eternal realities in all of existence.

- Taoism's focus on nature and ritual, rather than creeds and doctrines, distinguishes it from the Abrahamic monotheisms of Judaism, Christianity, and Islam.

THE DHARMACHAKRA, PAGE 77

Buddhism

Buddhism developed in India in the 6th century BCE, and it is focused on the life and teachings of a man named Siddhartha Gautama, who eventually became known by the title "Buddha" or "enlightened one." Gautama gathered disciples and taught them his philosophy and methods; they and those who came after them carried his teachings throughout southeast Asia and, eventually, to the rest of the world. Because Siddhartha was born a Hindu, Buddhism contains many of Hinduism's root ideas, such as karma and reincarnation. However, Buddhism departs from its Hindu roots in significant ways.

In many places, such as China and Japan, Buddhism blends easily with indigenous traditions like Taoism and Shinto. Like most global religions, Buddhism takes on the traits of the culture in which it finds itself, so it can look very different from country to country. That said, the core of Buddhist teaching and practice is that suffering in human life comes from the extreme craving that dominates our minds when they are ignorant or undisciplined.

The way to alleviate that suffering is to educate and train the mind through study and meditation.

Buddhist meditation techniques can be as complicated or as simple as one wants. Buddhism contains some of the most complex philosophies of the mind and consciousness that humans have ever developed. At the same time, Buddhism offers the simplest, easiest practices for anyone, anywhere to begin training their mind toward enlightenment and reduced suffering. This is one reason why some people have tacked on Buddhist meditation practices to other religious traditions that have very little in common with Buddhism. Others, especially in the West, have adapted Buddhist meditation techniques for completely secular purposes, like pain management and stress reduction. In these ways, Buddhism has become a truly global religion that fascinates and attracts people from all walks of life.

Cheat Sheet

When it began: 6th century BCE

Number of adherents: about 500 million

Percentage of world population: about 7 percent

Primary location: Asian-Pacific countries, including China, Thailand, and Japan

Largest sect/denomination: Mahayana

Primary text: *Tripitaka*, a collection of texts from the first centuries of Buddhism, written in the Pali language

Most recognizable symbol: statues of the Buddha, the lotus flower, and the dharmachakra (page 70)

KEY DATES

6th CENTURY BCE	Siddhartha Gautama, who came to be called the Buddha, lives (scholars debate the actual dates; some place him as late as the 3rd century BCE).
273– 236 BCE	The reign of Ashoka, king of the Mauryan Empire. He converts to Buddhism and helps it spread throughout India and into Sri Lanka.
250 BCE	The third of three councils, this one called by Ashoka, determines the *Tripitaka* ("Three Baskets") as a canon of Buddhist scripture.
300 BCE– 100 CE	Rise of the dominant Buddhist schools of thought: Theravada and Mahayana. Buddhism spreads to south-east Asia.
1st CENTURY CE	Buddhism spreads to China.
2nd–3rd CENTURY	Nagarjuna, prominent Buddhist philosopher and founder of the Madhyamika school of Buddhism, lives.
5th CENTURY	Bodhidharma, founder of Chan Buddhism in China (later known as Zen Buddhism in Japan), lives.
5th–6th CENTURY	Asanga, philosopher and founder of Yogacara school of Buddhism, lives.
6th CENTURY	Buddhism comes to Japan from Korea.
8th CENTURY	Vajrayana Buddhism is established in Tibet, largely through the work of missionary Padmasambhava.
9th CENTURY	Borobudur, a Mahayana temple/stupa complex, which is the largest Buddhist temple in the world, is constructed.
13th CENTURY	Zen, Pure Land, and Nichiren Buddhism are established in Japan.
1893	At the World Parliament of Religions in Chicago, Illinois, Buddhism and other Asian-originated religions gain massive public exposure to Western audiences.
1989	Tenzin Gyatso, the 14th Dalai Lama of Tibet, wins the Nobel Peace Prize.

On the Buddhist Calendar

PARINIRVANA (NIRVANA DAY)

February

A festival that celebrates the death of the Buddha, which is synonymous with his entrance into nirvana. Celebrants gather at temples or monasteries for meditation, charitable gift-giving, and meals.

AVALOKITEŚVARA'S BIRTHDAY

Spring, summer, and fall (in the northern hemisphere)

Celebrations for this famous Buddhist bodhisattva occur three times a year in various countries. People usually come to the temple with cakes and fresh flowers to make offerings to statues of her and to meditate.

VESAK (BUDDHA DAY)

May

This holiday happens on the first full moon in May every year and celebrates the birth, enlightenment, and death of the Buddha. The term *"Vesak"* refers to the Indian month of his birth. Celebrants gather in temples to meditate, make offerings, "bathe" statues of the Buddha, and eat vegetarian food.

BODHI DAY

December

This generally quiet holiday celebrates the Buddha sitting under the bodhi tree and achieving enlightenment. People gather in the temple for chanting and meditation, and they may meet in small groups for tea. Some decorate fig or fir trees to commemorate the legendary bodhi tree.

Burning Questions

WHO WAS THE BUDDHA?

The Buddha's given name was Siddhartha Gautama, and he lived in the 6th century BCE. Tradition holds that he was a prince set to inherit his father's kingdom when he had a spiritual crisis and, in accordance with Hindu tradition, left his home and family to become a *sannyasi*, or "forest dweller." He learned from Hindu and possibly also Jain teachers, practiced various austerities, and studied the ways that Hinduism instructed, but none of these helped him achieve his spiritual goals. Finally, he sat down under a bodhi tree to meditate alone. After several weeks, during which he went into trance states, experienced terrifying visions, and endured painful inner battles, he achieved enlightenment. He gathered disciples and began to teach what he'd come to see as the truth of reality.

He spent the next 45 years teaching this truth, called *dharma* in Buddhism, to his disciples and followers and setting up the basic ideas of what would become the Buddhist *sangha,* or community. He lived to around age 80 and, according to Buddhist belief, passed into nirvana—which means "extinguishment" or "nothingness"—thus escaping the cycle of life, death, and rebirth.

What he left behind is called the Triple Treasure: the Buddha (his life and example), the *dharma* (teachings and doctrine), and the *sangha* (the community of practitioners).

The term "Buddha" is a title which means "enlightened one." After he achieved enlightenment under the bodhi tree, according to the tradition, this title became appropriate for him.

WHY DIDN'T THE BUDDHA FIND WHAT HE WAS LOOKING FOR IN HINDUISM?

The traditional stories say that two aspects of Hindu practice at that time failed him: one was too philosophical and theoretical, and the other was too austere. This second practice—the practice of austerities like fasting from food and drink and going without sleep—especially failed him, according to the traditional stories about his quest.

One story says that each day, during the height of his attempts to achieve enlightenment through the austerities common in Jainism and some forms of Hinduism at the time, he ate only one grain of rice and drank only one drop of water. Some Buddhist iconography presents Siddhartha during this period in his quest as severely emaciated. He later taught that while practicing austerities, he was no more able to meditate or focus on achieving enlightenment than he had been back in his younger years in his father's palace, eating rich food and drinking fine wine. Both practices—severe asceticism and intense indulgence—left him sleepy and lethargic.

Hence, the Buddhist path is sometimes called "the middle way"—a middle path between extreme indulgence and extreme asceticism. Eat, exercise, and rest enough to stay healthy so that you can meditate properly and effectively.

YOU SAY THE BUDDHA IS THE "ENLIGHTENED ONE" AND HE ACHIEVED ENLIGHTENMENT UNDER THE BODHI TREE. WHAT IS THE TRUTH HE ACHIEVED?

The most basic collection of Buddhist teaching is called the Four Noble Truths. All schools of Buddhism affirm these Four Noble Truths as, indeed, noble and true—and the heart of the Buddha's teaching. These four truths contain the essence of what the Buddha came to know as he achieved enlightenment under the bodhi tree. The truths are:

1. All of life involves suffering—even the most privileged of human lives includes suffering of some sort.

2. Suffering is mostly caused by the mind's craving—its unenlightened desire for things to be other than what they are.

3. Suffering can be minimized or eliminated by enlightening the mind's desires.

4. The Eightfold Path toward achieving the enlightenment of the mind. Much of Buddhist teaching and practice can be seen as fulfilling one or more aspects of this path. This path is often represented by the eight spokes of the dharmachakra (page 70), also known as the wheel of chakra.

HOW DID BUDDHISM SPREAD?

Buddhism spread the way many religions spread: through human migration, trade routes, and natural increase. Specifically, Buddhism enjoyed imperial support in its homeland of India, as well as in China a few hundred years later. In the 3rd century BCE, India's Emperor Ashoka adopted Buddhist teachings for himself and sent monks throughout India and beyond to spread Buddhist teachings. In China, the Tang dynasty (7th to 10th centuries) is considered a "golden age" for Buddhism's development, when the religion spread largely because of imperial support. Finally, in some instances, cultural appropriation was a mechanism for spread, as in the case of Japan's almost wholesale importing of Chinese culture during the Heian period (8th to 12th centuries).

WHAT DOES THE BUDDHA MEAN WHEN HE SAYS THAT IGNORANT DESIRE CREATES SUFFERING?

Another way to describe ignorant desire is craving. In English, "craving" carries a stronger meaning than simply "desire." Ignorant desire is a kind of craving experienced by the mind. The Buddha taught that our mind, when unenlightened about the nature of reality, craves things that are nearly impossible to achieve. It wants things to last forever, even though they won't. It wants permanent happiness to come from the possession of impermanent things, even though it won't. It grasps and clings to things, trying to control them and never lose them, when it can't really control anything but itself. When our craving mind fails in all these attempts, we suffer. Therefore, the Buddha taught that enlightening the mind was the way to reduce and even eliminate suffering. The cause of suffering is not something or someone outside of us; it is within us. It is our own mind.

DOES BUDDHISM BELIEVE IN KARMA AND REINCARNATION LIKE HINDUISM?

Yes, Buddhism incorporates these two core ideas from Hinduism. Both religions teach that karma is an energy that accompanies actions of moral significance and that karmic energy follows people through their many lives until it is neutralized. Reincarnation, for both religions, is a cyclical understanding of time in which individuals exist perpetually in a cycle of life, death, and rebirth until they escape that cycle through spiritual practices.

DO BUDDHISTS REVERE A GOD OR THE GODS OF HINDUISM?

Not really. Buddhism is, at its core, an atheistic religion—meaning "no god." Buddhism generally does not name worship of a god or deity as a key to achieving nirvana or as central to taming unenlightened desire. Some iconography of the Buddha under the bodhi tree show him receiving the Hindu gods after he achieved enlightenment. In these depictions, the Hindu gods bow at his feet, ready to receive his teachings so that they, too, can escape the cycle of life, death, and rebirth and enter into nirvana. So, the Buddha is not a god to be revered the way the deities of Hinduism, Judaism, Christianity, or Islam are worshipped.

That said, there are sects within Buddhism—for example, Pure Land Buddhism in Japan— whose practices come close to looking like worship of the Buddha as a god. Moreover, in many parts of Mahayana Buddhism, certain figures known as *bodhisattvas* are revered and worshipped as holy, mainly because they are believed to be people who have achieved full enlightenment or "Buddha nature" but have chosen to stay in this life in order to teach others the way. Bodhisattvas are not gods, but they possess Buddha nature, which is the most highly respected and revered thing in Buddhism.

HOW IS BUDDHISM DIFFERENT FROM HINDUISM, GIVEN THAT BUDDHA HIMSELF WAS BORN A HINDU?

Buddhism, as previously stated, incorporates the core ideas of karma and reincarnation found in Hinduism. They differ, however, in what happens exactly when karma is neutralized and people escape the cycle of life, death, and rebirth. For Hindus, generally speaking, once a person achieves release from the cycle of life, death, and rebirth, their soul (atman) remerges with the world soul (Brahman). In Buddhism, there is no permanent soul or atman. Instead, there is a "self" that is propelled from life to life through the energy of karma, and when that karma is neutralized through spiritual work that results in enlightenment, the self passes into nirvana, or extinguishment.

In short, Buddhists and Hindus differ on the nature of the self (permanent or not) and on what happens upon being released from the cycle of life, death, and rebirth. Also, Buddhist methods for achieving liberation and enlightenment are different. For example, in Buddhism, worship of or devotion to a deity plays little role in achieving enlightenment, which stands in contrast to some dominant forms of Hinduism.

Finally, Buddhism isn't as deeply rooted in its geographic origins as Hinduism. The bulk of Hinduism's development as a religion has taken place in India and is marked definitively by Indian culture, whereas Buddhism's historical development has taken place in many areas of Southeast Asia, so the religion's major movements and schools reflect those many different cultures.

WHAT ARE THE MAIN SCHOOLS OF THOUGHT IN BUDDHISM?

There are three main schools of thought within Buddhism. The oldest is Theravada, meaning "Doctrine of the Elders," which developed not long after the life of the Buddha and is dominant in Sri Lanka, Myanmar, and other places in Southeast Asia. Its adherents focus on the individual pursuit of nirvana through mostly monastic practices.

Next is the Mahayana, meaning "Great Vehicle," which developed partially in response to Theravada. The Mahayana school emphasizes the *bodhisattva*, an individual who achieves enlightenment but, instead of

Everyday Buddhism

Being "Zen"

Zen Buddhism developed in 13th-century Japan and is the Japanese version of Chan Buddhism, which developed in China during the Tang dynasty. It is a school of thought and practice within Mahayana Buddhism that teaches the core ideas of Buddhism. However, Zen Buddhism emphasizes a form of meditation rooted in theories of the mind that are studied today in the discipline of psychology.

Because of this special psychological aspect, Zen Buddhist teaching has found a welcome audience in the West among not just those who self-identify as Buddhists but a broader swath of people who wish to manage their destructive thoughts and achieve more peace and happiness in their lives as well.

The term "zen" has come, in popular thought and speaking, to refer to a simple, calm, peaceful, and even minimalist way of being. To remain zen in the midst of chaos is to stay centered, calm, and present despite whatever is going on around you. Zen is the ultimate form of being "chill."

passing into nirvana, chooses to stay inside the cycle of life, death, and rebirth in order to help others. Mahayana is dominant in China and Japan. Many schools of thought and practice inside Buddhism, such as Zen or Pure Land, are major sects within Mahayana.

The third school of thought is Vajrayana, which means "Diamond Vehicle" or "Thunderbolt Vehicle." This is primarily Tibetan Buddhism and includes indigenous shamanic and tantric practices. Tantra emphasizes esoteric and secret rituals, texts, and meditative practices.

TELL ME MORE ABOUT A BODHISATTVA. WHO OR WHAT IS THAT?

In general, a bodhisattva is someone who has determined to become a buddha and is walking the path toward that goal. In much Mahayana Buddhism, however, the bodhisattva is someone who has already achieved enlightenment, or "Buddhahood," and, thus, has escaped the cycle of life, death, and rebirth (called samsara in Hinduism) and could pass into nirvana (nothingness, great bliss) for eternity. Instead, the bodhisattva chooses to stay in this cycle of life, death, and rebirth—all the while enlightened—in order to teach others and help them on their path to enlightenment. This is called the bodhisattva ideal, an ethical ideal of compassion for all sentient beings.

Several of the entities revered throughout Buddhism, in addition to the Buddha himself, are bodhisattvas. One of the most famous is Avalokiteśvara (also called Guanyin) in China. A contemporary person believed to be a bodhisattva is Tenzin Gyatso, the current Dalai Lama of Tibet. Tibetan Buddhists and others believe him to be the 14th incarnation in a line of spiritual leaders that traces back to Avalokiteśvara.

DO BUDDHISTS HAVE A PRIMARY SCRIPTURE OR TEXT THEY READ?

Buddhism ascribes to a large number of texts written over many hundreds of years. The first major sacred text, which is respected by most of the different Buddhist groups, is the *Tripitaka*, or "Three Baskets," which is a compilation of the Buddha's teachings, as well as commentary on those teachings arranged into three sections, or "baskets." The text was compiled via three formal councils of Buddhist monks, scholars, and political leaders sympathetic to Buddhism between the 5th and 3rd centuries BCE. Another important text is the *Buddhacarita*, composed by Ashvaghosha in the 2nd century, which tells the life story of the Buddha.

IS BUDDHISM MORE OF A PHILOSOPHY THAN A RELIGION?

Not really. Some people adopt a generally Buddhist view of life and attempt to enlighten their thinking in ways that help them be happy and free of stress in their lives. For such people, Buddhist ideas function similar to, say, the Stoic or Jungian ideas one might hear from a therapist or counselor. As we've seen, however, Buddhism is also very much a religion with temples, monks, sacred holidays and places, and a vast array of rituals and practices.

DO BUDDHISTS DO YOGA?

Not exactly. Yoga, for many Westerners, refers to the physical postures people use to stretch and stay limber. In religious and spiritual traditions, however, yoga can refer not only to physical postures accompanied by breathing exercises but also to mental exercises. Most major Buddhist schools of thought and practice do not emphasize or include physical postures (what Hindus call asanas), although some Buddhists informed by tantric practice may include these. Having said this, several martial arts traditions have been developed in Chinese Buddhist monasteries as ways for the monks to stay physically fit, optimize their mental strength, and boost their meditation practice. The Shaolin monks are the most famous in this tradition.

WHAT ABOUT THE STATUES THAT SHOW THE BUDDHA BEING FAT AND HAPPY?

The "happy Buddha" or "laughing Buddha" statues are a very common iconography of the Buddha, particularly in traditions informed by Chinese Buddhism. They are not designed to present the Buddha with historical accuracy; after all, he was a spiritual teacher who spent many years engaging in ascetic practices, like fasting, then spent the rest of his life eating and drinking only what was needed to keep his body healthy so that he would have the energy and alertness to meditate. Instead, these fat, happy Buddhas are symbols of Buddha nature—the enlightenment that Gautama attained that transformed him.

Everyday Buddhism

Meditation

Meditation is the primary spiritual practice in Buddhism and traces back to the Buddha himself as he sat in meditation under the bodhi tree and achieved enlightenment. Buddhism contains a vast array of meditation techniques and teachings, and each different school and sect prefers its own methods and perspectives on this central practice. Buddhists from all walks of life undertake meditation as a method of training and enlightening the mind.

The Buddha taught that suffering in our lives mainly stems from unenlightened cravings in the mind—that lust for permanence when all things are impermanent, that wish for things to last forever when all things will pass away. Meditation trains the mind so that it can see clearly through the illusions of unenlightened thinking.

Adept Buddhist monks can meditate for hours, not eating or drinking, barely even moving. Other Buddhists may only be able to meditate for a few minutes at a time, but perhaps they do it every day, day after day, week after week. Often, meditation is accompanied by chanting a *mantra*—a syllable, word, or phrase that aids the person in focusing their mind.

Sometimes meditation involves visualizing certain realities. Other times, meditation involves simply focusing on one's breath and trying to empty the mind of any thought. Again, Buddhist meditation runs the gamut between complex and simple and all points in between.

A basic interpretation is that the Buddha is "fat" with joy and compassion for all sentient beings. His rotund body is a symbol for what can happen when the mind is freed from ignorant cravings; people can become consumed by joy and compassion, even filled with it. Additionally, and more specifically, the laughing Buddha statues are often modeled upon a semi-historical monk named Budai, who was fat and jolly and came to be venerated as a Buddha, or enlightened one.

WHERE ARE THE MOST IMPORTANT SACRED SITES FOR BUDDHISTS?

There are many sacred or holy places for Buddhists. Most of them are associated with important events in the life of the historical Buddha or of *bodhisattvas* who are revered in a given country or region. A few sites in India are sacred because they connect to the Buddha's life. Bodh Gaya is holy because Buddhists view it as the place where Gautama sat under the bodhi tree to achieve enlightenment. It is believed that he gave his first sermon in Benares, India, and there is a large stupa (a special burial monument) there that commemorates that important moment. Kushinagar, the place in northern India where he died and passed into nirvana, is another holy site. His birthplace in Lumbini—not in India, but in nearby Nepal—is also holy.

DO BUDDHISTS HAVE TEMPLES OR OTHER SACRED BUILDINGS?

Yes, but they vary greatly between countries and reflect the cultures and communities in which they exist. Small neighborhood or "village" temples will have a different feel to them than the large temples connected to monasteries or those that anchor urban areas. Tibetan temples and Cambodian temples are designed differently because they come out of different cultural traditions. Chinese temples strongly resemble the imperial palace traditions of Chinese history.

Sacred spaces don't just reflect their country's architecture; they also reflect the particular brand of Buddhism practiced in that place. For example, Japanese Buddhist temples will reflect a form of Buddhism common in Japan, namely, Pure Land Buddhism. Temples outside of Japan aren't likely to resemble these Japanese temples. Additionally, in Japan, Buddhism has blended with the indigenous tradition of Shinto, so Japanese Buddhist temples may also feature aspects unique to Shinto that won't appear at all in Buddhist temples outside of Japan. Buddhist temples in the West often take on the architectural characteristics of Christian churches with benches, kneeling rails, racks for hymnals or other books, and so forth.

Finally, temples aren't the only kind of sacred space in Buddhism. Zen Buddhism, for example, makes extensive use of outdoor garden spaces alongside temples.

WHAT IS A STUPA?

A stupa is an ancient Indian burial monument that is shaped like an egg or a dome. In Buddhism, stupas of varying sizes have become a standard sacred architecture that often marks holy places. Stupas usually contain either the remains of a revered or honored person (a bodhisattva, for example) or relics associated with them. Stupas often have areas for meditation and worship attached to them and can be simple or ornate. The stupa at Sarnath in India, where it is believed the Buddha gave his first sermon, is several stories high but fairly simple in design. By contrast, the famous stupa at Borobudur in Indonesia is massive and one of the most ornately designed sacred spaces in the world.

HOW DO BUDDHIST CELEBRATIONS VARY ACROSS REGIONS?

Any country or region with a long-running connection to Buddhism has its own unique holidays and festivals. Holidays also vary within the various schools of Buddhist thought—some holidays are more prominent in Theravada communities, while others are more common in Mahayana communities. Vaishakha (or Vesak), for example, is celebrated mainly by Theravadists, as well as by Tibetan and Mongolian Buddhists and also some Hindus. At this major holiday, monks perform special rituals and teach in large public gatherings. This holiday traces back to Emperor Ashoka and commemorates Buddha's life as a whole.

Mahayana Buddhists in many countries celebrate Ancestor Day, also called "Ulambana" or "Ghost Festival," where they offer food to departed ancestors who appear as "hungry ghosts."

WHAT DOES THE LOTUS FLOWER SYMBOLIZE?

Lotus flowers are a species of water lily that grow in muddy water and mud. The flower blooms vibrantly out into the air, in sharp contrast to the mud and water in which it is rooted. This symbolizes the idea that Buddha nature emerges, beautiful and undefiled, even in the midst of the "muddiness" of worldly life. In the midst of *samsara*—the cycle of life, death and rebirth—the lotus can bloom with proper cultivation. Enlightenment can be achieved. Buddhist statuary and paintings often depict the Buddha and bodhisattvas sitting on lotus flowers to emphasize this idea.

ARE BUDDHISTS VEGETARIANS?

Some are, some aren't. Vegetarianism isn't a strong teaching across the various Buddhist groups and schools of thought. It isn't likely that the Buddha himself was a vegetarian, and he didn't teach it specifically. That said, the strong teaching in Buddhism for cultivating compassion for all sentient beings pushes some Buddhists toward vegetarianism. Out of compassion for animals—the fact that they can feel pain, in addition to their existence as beings in the cycle of life, death, and rebirth—some Buddhists choose not to kill and eat animals.

WHY DO SOME BUDDHISTS BECOME MONKS OR NUNS?

For the same reasons some in other traditions, like Christianity or Hinduism, become monks and nuns: to give themselves over almost exclusively to their spiritual pursuits. Everyday life—what Hinduism calls "householder" life—involves all sorts of daily responsibilities, such as earning a living, caring for children, attending to aging parents or relatives, fulfilling marriage obligations, and doing all the mundane tasks of living. Householder life often doesn't leave much room for personal pursuits, including spiritual ones. Therefore, some religions offer an alternative life path in which people abandon everyday life, renounce those pursuits, take new vows aligned with their chosen spiritual path, and live in a monastic community with others who have done the same.

Buddhist monks and nuns often wear simple robes and shave their heads as part of their renunciation of worldly pursuits. The robes vary in color from country to country, but they mostly reflect the dyes and traditions preferred in that area rather than any specific Buddhist teaching. The shaved head for both monks and nuns indicates their renunciation of popular beauty standards and worldly attachment to how one looks.

Buddhist monks and nuns spend their days in prayer, meditation, study, and mindful work that supports the community.

How Buddhism Relates to Other Major Religions

Buddhism has spread around the world, at least partially, because of its adaptability to the cultures and contexts in which it finds itself. Therefore, students of world religions can find deep connections between Buddhism and other religions that may seem, on the surface, to be very different from one another. Buddhism, as a case study, is a perfect example of how religions can adapt, adjust, and renew themselves in order to stay alive—all while preserving the core aspects of their teaching and practice.

- Hinduism respects Buddhism as an important part of Indian religion and even sees the Buddha himself as one of the incarnations of Vishnu, the great Hindu god of the cosmic order. Gandhi, the great 20th-century Hindu teacher and activist, spoke of the Buddha as an enlightened teacher who offered a valuable critique to the Hinduism of his time.

- Some who identify as Jewish or Christian, especially those who are drawn to the mystical or contemplative aspects of their own religions, might add certain Buddhist meditation techniques to their own prayer practices. Whereas Buddhists may orient those techniques toward Guanyin or the Buddha, Jews and Christians will orient them toward their God or to Jesus Christ.

- Buddhism, like Taoism and Confucianism, is ultimately concerned with the right practices that bring about enlightenment. This is in contrast to Western faiths that are principally concerned with the "right belief" in creeds and doctrines.

- Like several other religions, including Christianity, Islam, Taoism, and Hinduism, Buddhism has been impacted by political realities that influenced its spread and its ability to thrive in a region or country.

THE CHRISTIAN CROSS, PAGE 109

CHAPTER FIVE

Christianity

Christianity is the largest religion in the world, with over 2 billion adherents. It has almost 2,000 years of organized history and has been a global religion for hundreds of years. The visionary founder of Christianity was an itinerate Jewish rabbi named Jesus who hailed from the small town of Nazareth in northern Israel. He was a miracle worker, folk healer, and teacher who taught largely through simple stories and parables. He gathered disciples and other followers who eventually came to believe that he was the messiah and formed a movement around his teachings.

The movement spread throughout the Roman Empire and was eventually adopted by the empire itself. Then it began its spread throughout the world. Because Jesus and many of his disciples and early followers were Jewish, Christianity contains some of the core ideas of Judaism; however, it departs from its Jewish "parent religion" in significant ways.

Christianity's influence cannot be overstated because, indeed, it is the largest religion in the history of the world and has been the religion of numerous empires and countries that have wielded enormous cultural power. Like all other religions with such a long history and global reach, Christianity comprises a fascinating and complex matrix of practices and beliefs spread across its myriad divisions and subgroups.

Cheat Sheet

When it began: 1st century CE

Number of adherents: about 2.3 billion

Percentage of world population: about 32 percent

Primary location: primarily the northern hemisphere in the West (i.e., Europe, parts of the Middle East and Asia, North America). Increasingly, the center of gravity has shifted to the southern hemisphere in parts of Africa and Latin America

Largest sect/denomination: Catholic Christianity (about half of all Christians identify as Catholic)

Primary text: the Christian Bible or the Holy Bible

Most recognizable symbol: a cross (page 94) or a crucifix

KEY DATES

33 CE (ABOUT)	Death of Jesus.
64	Death of Paul the Apostle, an influential follower of Jesus.
272–337	Emperor Constantine of Rome, who supported Christianity as a legitimate religion of the empire, lives.
354–430	Augustine, the highly influential early theologian and leader whose ideas have shaped Christianity to this day, lives.
325	Council at Nicea (present-day Iznik, Turkey): a major meeting of Christian leadership convened by Emperor Constantine to settle matters of doctrine, specifically issues related to Jesus' human/divine nature. The doctrine of the Trinity was further established here.
367	Athanasius writes his "Easter Letter," in which he lists the accepted books of the Christian canon. Many scholars use this letter to help determine when the content of the Christian *Bible* was settled.
5th–6th CENTURIES	Rise of the importance of the bishopric of Rome, later called the Papacy.
1054	Schism between the western (Catholic) and eastern (Orthodox) parts of the church over various theological issues.
1225–1274	Thomas Aquinas, highly influential Catholic theologian, lives.
1483–1546	Martin Luther, the highly influential German Catholic monk whose criticisms of the Church sparked the Protestant Reformation and the founding of Lutheranism, lives.
1509–1564	John Calvin, the French theologian and reformer whose writings were some of the first systematic expositions of theology from the Protestant Reformation, lives.
1530s	King Henry VIII establishes the autonomy of the Church of England over and against the Catholic Church. Anglicanism is created and is part of the Protestant Reformation.
16th–20th CENTURIES	Nearly all Protestant denominations, including Baptists, Presbyterians, Congregationalists, Lutherans, Methodists, and Pentecostals, and all their subdivisions, are formed.

On the Christian Calendar

CHRISTMAS

December 25

Traditionally a winter festival that celebrates the birth of Jesus. People give gifts, decorate with lights and nativity scenes, which show Mary, the infant Jesus, and others from the biblical birth story. People may also decorate their homes with lights, candles, winter greenery, and Christmas trees. The holiday also features Santa Claus, a jolly white-haired man in a red suit who brings children gifts and whose history can be traced back to a 3rd-century Greek saint.

EPIPHANY

January 6

Also known as "Three Kings Day." For Orthodox Christians, this day celebrates Jesus' baptism; for other Christians, this holiday honors the day the wise men visited the infant Jesus. Some, like Armenian Christians, celebrate Christmas on this day. The 12 days between Christmas and Epiphany are the traditional "Twelve Days of Christmas" mentioned in the popular holiday song.

LENT

February to April

A 40-day period of penance and self-denial leading up to Easter. For branches of Orthodox Christianity, it usually lasts longer (depending on how they calculate it) and involves fasting (eating only one meal a day).

EASTER

March or April

A springtime holiday that celebrates the death and resurrection of Jesus. People attend services, share a meal, and adults may hide Easter eggs for children to find. The symbols of eggs, rabbits, and other such things point to Easter's coinciding with pre-Christian springtime festivals, which celebrate new life and "resurrection" from winter.

Burning Questions

WHY IS THE RELIGION CALLED "CHRISTIANITY"? WHAT DOES "CHRIST" MEAN?

The term "Christ" comes from the word *"christos,"* which is a Greek term for the Hebrew word that means "messiah." So, "Christ" is not Jesus' last name. Rather, it is a title given to Jesus by those who believe he is the messiah that was expected or hoped for by many Jewish groups in the 1st century CE. At the time, the dominant view of the coming messiah was that he would be a political figure to deliver or "save" the Jewish people from rule by the Greeks and Romans. Jesus didn't fit this description, so the claims of his messiahship were contentious. Ultimately, Christianity developed an entirely fresh understanding of the exact kind of "salvation" Jesus as the messiah provided.

WHO WAS JESUS?

Jesus was a Jewish man who lived in the 1st century CE in what is now the state of Israel. Not much is known for certain about his life, but the biblical tradition records that he was born in Bethlehem and raised in Nazareth— both small towns in central and northern Israel. His birth was miraculous, according to Christian belief, for his mother, Mary, was a virgin and became pregnant by divine power. As an adult, Jesus began his ministry as a healer, teacher, and miracle worker. For about three years, he traveled around what is now called Israel with his 12 disciples, gathering more and more followers as time passed.

His message was threatening to both Jewish and Roman authorities of the day, albeit for different reasons. The Romans were suspicious of any person who wasn't sufficiently respectful of the empire and its rulers, especially if that person gathered a following. The Jews feared that such a person from their community would draw unwanted attention and even persecution to themselves as a minority religious community. Jesus was sentenced by the Romans to death by crucifixion and was buried in a tomb. After three days, according to Christian belief, he rose from the dead and soon afterward ascended into heaven, leaving instructions for his disciples to spread his teaching of salvation—called the "gospel" or "good news"—to all the world.

HOW IS IT THAT CHRISTIANS BELIEVE THAT THERE IS ONLY ONE GOD, BUT THAT JESUS WAS DIVINE, TOO?

Christians believe in the Trinity, a doctrine which claims that there is one God who is expressed in three persons: God the Father, God the Son (Jesus), and God the Holy Spirit. The concept of the Trinity is one of the key differences between Christianity and both Judaism (its parent religion) and Islam (whose lineage also traces back to Judaism), which are staunch monotheisms that deny any other God but the one God of Abraham (the ancient Hebrew patriarch). Moreover, they deny that God could have a "son" or an alternative personage or form, such as the Holy Spirit.

The doctrine of the Trinity is also one of the most contested doctrines within the Christian faith. In the early centuries of the faith, religious leaders spent much time in official councils and meetings trying to hash out the doctrine theologically in order to affirm the divinity of Jesus and the Holy Spirit that he mentions, while simultaneously affirming the oneness of God. Probably the most famous council that focused on trinitarian doctrine was the Council at Nicea (in present-day Turkey) in 325 CE, which was convened by Roman emperor Constantine. The creed that was adopted in that council, called the Nicene Creed, is often viewed as a basic, foundational statement of the Christian faith and what it teaches. An earlier creed was called the Apostle's Creed. Both credal statements are still used today in various branches of Christianity.

WHAT ARE CHRISTIANITY'S MAIN SCRIPTURES?

The Christian Bible (also called the *Holy Bible*) is the primary sacred text in Christianity. It includes the Jewish scriptures (Torah, Prophets, Writings), which Christianity calls the "Old Testament," as well as a body of texts it calls the "New Testament." The term *"Bible"* generally refers to the standard version of the Protestant Bible, which differs slightly from the text used by Catholic and Orthodox Christians.

The Catholic Bible includes texts from a collection called the Apocrypha, meaning "hidden texts," that trace back to the Latin translation of the Bible in the 5th century CE. These apocryphal texts are not included in the Jewish canon of scripture or in any Protestant Bible after the Protestant Reformation of the 1500s.

A most notable version of the *Bible* is the King James Version of 1611, a translation that enlisted dozens of scholars working in groups to translate the texts into the English of the Elizabethan era. It was the dominant English translation of the *Bible* until the 20th century. Today, when scholars or students of literature use the term "biblical" to describe the prose of a novelist or poet, they are referring to the style of language in the King James Version of the *Bible*.

WHAT HAPPENED TO THE DISCIPLES THAT FOLLOWED JESUS WHILE HE WAS ALIVE?

According to the biblical record, one of the disciples, Judas Iscariot, betrayed Jesus just before his arrest and crucifixion and killed himself soon afterward. The others, according to the biblical account and stories in the early Christian tradition, spread out as missionaries from modern-day Israel into Turkey (what the biblical record calls "Asia Minor"), northern Africa, parts of east Asia (modern-day Russia and Armenia), and into current-day Iran, Iraq, and the Arabian Peninsula. Many of these areas were part of the Roman Empire or had long-established trade routes, so travel to far-off places was possible via land or sea with relative ease.

Many of the original disciples were killed for their faith and turned into martyrs by the faithful. A few seem to have lived out their lives in Christian communities that they themselves were instrumental in founding. John, for example, is claimed to have lived a long life in and around Ephesus, a city near the southwestern coast of modern-day Turkey. John, along with Peter and James, are viewed as Jesus' "inner circle" of disciples. Peter was executed via crucifixion by Emperor Nero of Rome in 66 CE, according to some records. James, according to the biblical record, was killed by King Herod, dying by the sword as the first disciple to be killed for his faith.

HOW DID CHRISTIANITY SPREAD?

Christianity has spread primarily through missionaries and by being championed by various powerful empires or countries. Jesus himself, in the biblical record, instructed his disciples and followers to spread his message around the world. The historical record seems to indicate that they did exactly this, and Christians have continued to spread the message of their faith via evangelism of various kinds for all of the religion's existence.

Additionally, as was the case with Buddhism, Islam, and other religions, Christianity enjoyed the patronage of powerful political entities at multiple points in its history. The Roman Empire, the Byzantine Empire, the British Empire, the Russian Empire, the Habsburg dynasty, and Spain and Portugal during the height of their political and colonial power all championed Christianity. Christianity was a favored religion in all of the geographic areas ruled by these empires, and, therefore, the religion's adherents faced no real pressure in growing, expanding, and establishing their faith. Finally, Christianity spreads by natural increase, as Christians have children and grandchildren, all of whom are then raised in the faith.

HOW IS CHRISTIANITY DIFFERENT FROM JUDAISM, SINCE JESUS HIMSELF WAS JEWISH?

The primary difference has to do with the person of Jesus himself. Christianity affirms Jesus as the messiah and as divine, which Judaism has never affirmed. Apart from this, Jesus' teachings challenged the Judaism of his day on issues like proper observance of Jewish laws and social codes. The biblical record tells of Jesus being questioned about why he didn't keep the Sabbath laws and why he ate and socialized with people who were considered "unclean" according to Jewish law, such as lepers and others.

Everyday Christianity

Church on Sundays

Many Christians observe their faith by joining other Christians in group worship at least once a week. That worship day, for many Christian groups, is on Sunday. While Catholic churches will hold services, called a Mass, on Saturday nights, and others may hold services throughout the week, Sunday is the day of the week most associated with a Christian "Sabbath." Until just a few decades ago in many parts of the West, stores, restaurants, and other retail outlets were closed on Sundays. Blue laws in some parts of the United States forbade the sale of certain items (like alcohol) on Sundays or limited the hours of the day in which they could be sold. Some states still limit the sale of alcohol on Sundays, though not explicitly for Sabbath-related reasons, but those reasons are part of the historical background to such laws.

The Christian faith's interpretation of Jesus' and Moses' death constituted another major break with Judaism. Traditional Christianity views Jesus' death not merely as a tragedy but as a sacrificial death that redeemed or "atoned for" the sins of all humankind. In essence, Jesus' death (and his blood) functions for all of humanity in a way similar to how the death of sacrificial animals (and their blood) functioned for Jews during the temple period of their history. In temple Judaism, people brought animals to the priests for them to sacrifice as an offering to God. Often, the blood of sacrificial animals was believed to redeem or atone for sin. This basic thinking gets applied to Jesus' death and blood in Christianity. What gives Jesus' death the power to save and redeem is the fact that he is not only a human; he is also divine. Judaism does not accept that Jesus is divine.

WHY DON'T CHRISTIANS HAVE THE KOSHER DIETARY CODES THAT JEWS HAVE?

In the years after Jesus' death, the issue of eating according to Jewish dietary codes (see "Everyday Judaism" page 33), as well as eating meat from animals that had been sacrificed to Greek or Roman gods, was a big topic of discussion and debate among many leaders in the Christian community.

The biblical record presents Jesus' followers Peter and Paul as having taken up this issue and even arguing about it at times. Peter had a vision in which he was instructed by God to eat animals that his Jewish faith had taught him were unclean. Paul came to believe that eating meat offered to Roman or Greek gods, or eating outside the traditional Jewish dietary codes, was permissible for Christians, mainly because Jesus' death and resurrection theologically changed the need to keep the Jewish law. Jesus' death, in Paul's view (which later became the accepted Christian view), revealed that human beings could never fully please God or achieve their own salvation through adherence to the Jewish law. It was only through the grace of God, and God's sending of his Son to die in order to redeem from sin, that humanity could be saved. So, the dietary codes lost their importance throughout most of Christianity, beginning from about the 2nd century CE.

YOU SAY THAT JESUS' DEATH IS A "SAVING" DEATH. HOW DO CHRISTIANS ACKNOWLEDGE OR PRACTICE THIS?

In addition to celebrating Easter, the holiday that commemorates Jesus' death and resurrection, most Christians honor Jesus' death through a ceremonial drinking of wine (or grape juice) and bread. According to the biblical account, during the Last Supper that Jesus shared with his disciples before he was arrested and crucified, he took wine and bread, held it out to them, and instructed them to drink and eat because it was his blood and body broken for them. Most Christians interpret this episode as Jesus referring to the sacrificial death he would soon experience.

Catholic and Orthodox liturgies, as well as some
Protestant liturgies, include a ritual drinking of wine
and eating of bread as a reenactment of this Last
Supper and of the sacrificial death of Jesus. Other
Protestants commemorate Jesus' death in a similar way,
but usually not as often (maybe once a month or once a
quarter, as opposed to every week for Catholics). Also,
many Protestant groups differ from Catholic and
Orthodox groups on what happens to the bread and the
wine in those ceremonial observances. The Catholic
church, for example, teaches a doctrine called "tran-
substantiation" whereby the bread and wine undergo a
change in substance, changing mystically into the literal
flesh and blood of Jesus. Most Protestants teach that
the bread and wine are symbols only and do not change
substance.

WHY DO SOME CHRISTIANS WEAR A CROSS OR CRUCIFIX NECKLACE OR HANG ONE UP ON THE WALL?

Most Christians commemorate the crucifixion of Jesus
as a defining event for human history. Protestants tend
to commemorate Jesus' death with a simple cross,
whereas Catholics and Orthodox Christians use a crucifix—a cross with a small statue (or an image, in the
case of the Orthodox) of Jesus hanging on the cross
from his hands and feet. This difference is primarily
due to the Protestant view of statues in the context of
worship. Protestantism generally rejects the use of statues in Christian worship and tends to see it as a form of

Everyday Christianity

A Cross to Wear

The cross (page 94) or crucifix is the most recognizable symbol in Christianity. In addition to adorning buildings, altars, and other spaces in the religion, many believers wear the cross or crucifix on a necklace. For many, this is a sign of their Christian faith; however, some who are not Christian, or who are only nominally so, wear a cross as a sign of a general belief in God or as a basic form of spirituality.

The cross, particularly in Western culture, has taken on a larger cultural significance that points to respect for religious faith overall, in addition to any faith one might have in Jesus as the Christ or the importance of his death on the cross.

idolatry. Older forms of Christianity, like Catholicism and Orthodox, do not share that view. So, any cross with a statue or image of Jesus on it will be accepted by Catholics and Orthodox but rejected by Protestants. A plain cross will be accepted by nearly all Christians.

WHAT'S THE DIFFERENCE BETWEEN CATHOLIC AND PROTESTANT CHRISTIANS?

Catholicism is one of the oldest forms of Christianity and is oriented around the authority and leadership of the bishop of Rome, who came to be called the Pope beginning in the 5th and 6th centuries. The Catholic church is hierarchically structured with bishops, priests, and others arranged in layers of authority under the Pope. Catholic worship is liturgical (following a set script of priest-led prayers, readings, chants, singing, etc.) and sacramental (attributing divine power to certain rituals like baptism, Eucharist, marriage, etc.).

Protestantism began in the 15th and 16th centuries as a reaction against what it deemed abuses and errors by the Catholic Church and its leadership. Most famously, the German monk Martin Luther nailed a list of grievances against the Catholic Church onto the door of a chapel in Wittenberg. The *Ninety-five Theses* became a catalyst for the Protestant Reformation.

Protestant denominations tend to have less hierarchical forms of organization and often allow regional or local congregations to manage their own affairs. Greater autonomy is granted to individual believers to interpret scripture and worship according to their own preferences. Protestant theology developed alongside political movements that replaced monarchies with nation-states ruled by representative governments. So, as Catholicism mirrors the hierarchical structures of the monarchies of its era, Protestantism mirrors the democratic hierarchies of its time.

WHO ARE ORTHODOX CHRISTIANS?

Orthodox Christianity, also called Eastern Orthodoxy, takes its name from the late 4th century, when the Roman Empire was divided into western and eastern sections. The western empire was more Latin in culture, whereas the eastern was more Greek or Hellenistic. While the western empire faded under attack by Visigoth tribes, the eastern empire transitioned to be called the Byzantine Empire and remained largely intact for several more centuries. The Christian communities in the west and the east developed in divergent theological directions until they finally split in 1054 CE over a variety of theological issues, including the authority of the bishop of Rome, whom western Christians called the Pope. The western form of Christianity became known as the Roman Catholic Church, and the eastern form became known as the Orthodox. Both have hierarchical forms of government and are theologically sacramental. Orthodoxy is a dominant form of Christianity in large parts of the Middle East, Russia, Greece, Turkey, Eastern Europe, and parts of northern Africa (Egypt in particular).

YOU MENTION THE "SACRAMENTS" OR SOME CHRISTIAN WORSHIP BEING "SACRAMENTAL." WHAT DOES THAT MEAN?

A sacrament, in Christian theology, is a ritual or sacred event that involves the direct experience of the divine or the direct imparting of divine grace. As such, a sacrament is a window or channel through which the human and divine connect. In Catholic and Orthodox traditions, as well as in a handful of the oldest Protestant traditions (i.e., Anglican, Lutheran), the most observed sacraments are baptism and Eucharist (the ritual eating of bread and wine associated with Jesus' body and blood). Confirmation—when a person confesses Jesus as the Christ as a confirmation of their baptism—is also one of the traditional sacraments of the Catholic and Orthodox communities, as well as some Protestants. Marriage, ordination, penance, and anointing the sick join baptism, Eucharist, and confirmation to make the traditional seven sacraments of the Church. Most Protestant denominations perform baptism, some sort of Eucharist service (also called "communion"), marriage, ordination, and other such rituals. However, Protestants (with some exceptions) don't tend to have a sacramental understanding of these rituals because they don't view them as ritual channels of direct, divine grace or power.

DO ALL CHRISTIAN GROUPS HAVE PRIESTS?

Not exactly. "Priest" is a term usually used to refer to clergy in Orthodox, Catholic, or Anglican (Episcopalian) branches of Christianity. Most Protestants refer to their clergy as a minister, pastor, or preacher rather than a priest. "Deacon" is a term that has more crossover use among the different branches of the religion. In Catholic, Orthodox, and Anglican branches, deacons are ordained, professional clergy who can perform a subset of the ritual functions that a priest can perform. In Protestantism, deacons aren't necessarily ordained (although they might be); they function more like a board of trustees or a board of elders to guide and govern a local church.

WHAT DOES CHRISTIANITY TEACH ABOUT THE AFTERLIFE?

Christianity, in general, affirms the existence of an afterlife of either blessing or suffering based on one's faith during earthly life. Eternal reward and punishment, in either heaven or hell, has a long and convoluted history throughout Christianity. Some groups de-emphasize eternal punishment in hell for various reasons. Overall, most Christians believe in or hope for an afterlife in a heaven or in the presence of God and Christ, and they believe that their deceased loved ones are in the presence of God.

WHAT ARE THE MAIN HOLIDAYS IN CHRISTIANITY, OTHER THAN CHRISTMAS?

Easter is the oldest and most significant Christian holiday, and it is celebrated by nearly all Christians. Whereas Christmas celebrates Jesus' birth, Easter celebrates his resurrection from the dead. Many Christians also celebrate Lent or the Lenten season, the season leading up to Jesus' death, as well as the season leading up to his birth, called Advent. Additionally, within these seasons are various important holy days. For example, Good Friday is the day of Jesus' crucifixion before his resurrection on Easter Sunday. Ash Wednesday is the first day of Lent, which begins six weeks before Easter. Epiphany is celebrated on January 6 and, for most Christians, marks the biblical story of the wise men's visiting of the baby Jesus.

BESIDES JESUS, WHO ARE THE MOST IMPORTANT PEOPLE IN CHRISTIANITY?

Most scholars say Paul the Apostle, an early convert to Jesus' message and movement, is the most important person after Jesus in the history of the Christian faith. Some even say that Paul is a founder of the faith because he, more than almost any other early follower of Jesus, did the theological and administrative heavy lifting to get the movement established, which helped it endure the persecutions and other hardships the early Christian communities experienced.

Paul was not one of the original 12 disciples who traveled with Jesus. In fact, Paul never met Jesus personally. Instead, Paul had a mystical encounter with Jesus that caused him to believe that Jesus was the messiah, and he used his training as a Jewish leader and teacher to interpret Jesus' death and preach the gospel to other Jews as well as to Gentiles (non-Jews). Paul's missionary journeys were some of the first major events through which the Christian faith spread. Moreover, two-thirds of the Bible's New Testament comprises Paul's letters to Christian groups in Corinth, Ephesus, Rome, Galatia, and elsewhere.

WHAT IS A "GOSPEL"?

The term "gospel" is an English rendering of the Greek word "euangelion" (or the Latin "evangelium"), which means "good news." In Christianity, the term "gospel" refers to two distinct things. First, it refers to the general "good news" that Jesus preached, as well as the "good news" of what Christians believe his death and resurrection accomplished for humankind. Secondly, the term "gospel" is used to describe the genre of literature of the first four books of the New Testament—the gospels of Matthew, Mark, Luke, and John. These four gospels are named after four of Jesus' disciples and are the primary texts that provide details of the life and ministry of Jesus. Additional gospels were written about Jesus from the 1st century onward, but they were not included in the New Testament for various reasons.

I'VE HEARD OF THE HOLY SPIRIT—
WHAT OR WHO IS THAT?

The Holy Spirit is the third person of the Trinity in Christian theology and, as such, is seen as divine. The Holy Spirit is also called the "Comforter," which refers to a gospel passage in which Jesus tells his disciples that, after he leaves them, he will send the "Comforter," or the Holy Spirit, to be with them and guide them.

Acts of the Apostles in the New Testament tells of the Holy Spirit coming to the disciples, an event that is celebrated in a holiday called Pentecost in many Christian traditions. Some scholars trace the Christian Holy Spirit back to the spirit of God mentioned in Jewish texts that was present at creation and is a guide toward divine wisdom.

DO CHRISTIANS REVERE ALL THE JEWISH SCRIPTURES?

Yes, in general. The sections of scripture that Judaism identifies as Torah, Prophets, and Writings make up what Christianity calls the Old Testament, which is the first major section of the Christian Bible. However, Jews also respect the Talmud, a collection of rabbinic interpretations of the Jewish sacred texts. Christians do not revere the Talmud in the ways that Jews do.

I'VE SEEN STATUES OF SAINTS AND ANGELS. WHO ARE THEY?

For Christians, angels are supernatural beings who populate the heavenly realms, including the realm of the presence of God. Even though Christian lore holds that Satan was an angel who rebelled against God, Christians tend to think of angels in positive terms, usually as messengers, guardians, or helpers sent by God. The angel Gabriel figures prominently in the birth story of Jesus, and unnamed angels appear in the apocalyptic narrative of *The Revelation* in the New Testament, which tells of the end of the world and a final judgment.

The term "saint" may mean slightly different things to Protestants, Catholics, and the Orthodox. To Protestants, the term "saint" can apply to anyone inside the faith, living or dead, who is living (or lived) a committed Christian life. But Catholic and Orthodox branches of Christianity take this a step further by officially recognizing, or canonizing, certain deceased individuals, thus giving them the title of "saint." People inside these branches of the religion may use icons or statues of the saints in their prayers.

Usually, in order to be sainted, a person needs to have performed miracles during their lifetime and lived a life of extraordinary holiness or service to God and others. Catholics and Orthodox do not recognize each other's saints that were canonized after the schism between the groups in 1054 CE. Some Protestants (Anglicans and Lutherans mainly) will acknowledge the sainthood of some individuals, but, in general, Protestantism doesn't emphasize saints and doesn't use iconography or statues of them in prayer or worship. Protestantism, as a whole, tends to be iconoclastic—against the use of statues in worship.

How Christianity Relates to Other Major Religions

Historically, Christianity is the "middle" religion between Judaism and Islam—the three main Abrahamic monotheisms. As such, it retains some core concepts from its parent religion and also passes down certain ideas to Islam. Together, these three religions—especially Christianity and Islam—are a huge presence in the world simply because of their sheer size and number. More than half of the world's population practices either Christianity or Islam.

- Hindus and Buddhists generally respect Jesus—not as divine, in the way that Christians do, but as a spiritual leader worthy of respect and a sage whose teachings offer benefit for those wishing to make progress on their own spiritual paths.

- Jesus was Jewish, and he, much like Lao tzu and the Buddha, had an interesting relationship to the religion founded upon his teachings. Jesus was not a Christian, Lao tzu was not a Taoist, and the Buddha was not a Buddhist—mainly because those religions as organized entities with rituals, doctrines, clergy, and priesthoods didn't exist during their lifetimes.

- Judaism, Christianity, Islam, and Sikhism are monotheisms, even though the Christian doctrine of the Trinity speaks of one deity in three persons.

- In general, both Christianity and Islam affirm the belief in eternal reward and punishment and, by extension, the existence of heaven and hell. Some aspects of Christian doctrine teach that those who do not believe in Jesus as the Christ will suffer eternally in hell. The more traditional and conservative groups tend to affirm this teaching. Many Christian groups, however, don't emphasize this teaching, and some don't agree with it or teach it at all.

THE CRESCENT AND STAR, PAGE 133

CHAPTER SIX

Islam

Islam is the second largest religion in the world and has followers on every continent. Historically, it is the third of the major monotheisms that trace their theological lineages back to Abraham, a figure who is first mentioned in the Jewish scriptures. Islam's central figure, other than Allah (Arabic for "God"), is Muhammad, the founder of the religion. Muslims believe Muhammad to be the final prophet sent by God to reveal truth to all of humanity.

Islam is a truly global religion and began spreading beyond its place of origin in the Arabian Peninsula almost immediately after Muhammad's death in the 7th century CE. Islam, like any global religion, has taken on the cultural patterns of the places where it has spread, so Islam in Indonesia or China looks very different from Islam in Saudi Arabia or Turkey. Within such cultural flexibility, however, is a core set of beliefs and practices that remain constant throughout the various permutations of the faith. Islam is a truly remarkable religion in this regard and offers a powerful case study in maintaining the tension between unity and diversity. Finally, despite being an iconoclastic religion—that is, forbidding figural art in sacred spaces—Islamic art and architecture is some of the most recognizable and beautiful in the world.

Cheat Sheet

When it began: early 7th century CE

Number of adherents: about 1.8 billion

Percentage of world population: just over 24 percent

Primary location: after beginning in the Arabian Peninsula, it spread quickly to Africa, Asia, and parts of Europe, and it is now a global religion with adherents everywhere

Largest sect/denomination: Sunni, which 85 percent of Muslims identify as

Primary text: the *Quran*; a secondary text is the *Hadith*

Most recognizable symbol: the crescent and star (page 120)

KEY DATES

570–632 CE	Muhammad, Islam's founder and final prophet, lives.
632–661	Period of the Caliphs: associates of Muhammad who led the Muslim community after he died. Islam begins to spread out from the Arabian Peninsula into the Mediterranean and Mesopotamian areas.
650 (ABOUT)	The *Quran* is written down and compiled under caliph Uthman.
661–750	Umayyad dynasty: the first Muslim dynasty, centered in Damascus. It spread Islam as far west as Spain and France and as far east as India.
750–1258	Abbasid dynasty, centered in Baghdad.
1058–1111	Al-Ghazali, a highly influential Muslim philosopher and scholar, lives.
909–1171	Fatimid dynasty, a Shi'ite dynasty in Egypt.
980–1037	Ibn Sina (Avicenna), a highly influential Iranian physician and philosopher, lives.
1099	Christian crusaders take Jerusalem from Muslims.
1126–1198	Ibn Rushd (Averroes), an influential philosopher, jurist, theologian from Cordova, Spain, lives.
11th–13th CENTURIES	Islam spreads and establishes itself throughout Africa and Asia. The Sufi brotherhoods are also founded.
1207–1273	Jalal ad-Din Muhammad Rumi (Rumi), an Afghan jurist and philosopher who has become one of the most famous poets in the world, lives.
1300–1922	Ottoman Empire: the Turkish Muslim empire reaches its height under the reign of Suleyman the Magnificent (1520 to 1566).
1452	Ottoman Mehmet Fatih conquers Constantinople, renames it Istanbul.
16th–19th CENTURIES	Mughal Empire in India.
19th–20th CENTURIES	Large numbers of Muslims come to the United States— first as slaves, and later as immigrants from Asia, Africa, and India.
1979	Iranian Revolution: the first attempt at a Muslim state in the modern world.

On the Islamic Calendar

RAMADAN

During the month of Ramadan, Muslims engage in fasting from all food and drink from dawn until sunset each day. Families and friends gather in groups for breakfast before dawn and for fast-breaking *iftars*, or dinners, after dark throughout the month. Because the Muslim calendar is lunar, the date of Ramadan shifts from year to year, as do all the celebrations and observances described here.

EID AL-FITR

Also known as the "Festival of Breaking the Fast," this two- to three-day event marks the end of Ramadan. It is celebrated by giving gifts, giving to charity, and gathering with friends to share meals.

EID AL-ADHA

The "Feast of the Sacrifice" marks the end of the days of annual pilgrimage to Mecca, which Muslims are encouraged to do at least once in their lifetimes. It includes several days of feasting and celebration. During this time, an animal—often a goat, sheep, or camel—is sacrificed as a reminder of the sacrifice Abraham was asked to make of his son by Allah. (For Muslims, it was Ishmael whom Abraham almost sacrificed, not Isaac, as the Jewish and Christian traditions assert.) The meat from the animal is eaten and shared with the poor.

Burning Questions

WHO WAS MUHAMMAD?

Muhammad was the visionary founder of Islam and the first leader of those who came to adopt the religion. He was born in Mecca and, after being orphaned at a young age, was raised by an uncle in a prominent Bedouin tribe. As an adult, he was a successful merchant who traveled the trade routes between oases across the Arabian Peninsula, working for his employer, a wealthy widow named Khadija. She was so impressed with Muhammad that she asked him to marry her, and he did.

In his forties, Muhammad had a series of spiritual experiences in a cave near Mecca that he understood to mean he was called to be a prophet of the one true God. He then began his work as the founder and leader of what became the religion of Islam. He did this work for over 20 years, continuing to have revelatory spiritual experiences, defending the young community of believers against those who renounced and attacked them, and teaching his close associates the message he claimed to have received from God. In the study of religions, he is a remarkable figure because he ended up wearing many hats during the decades after he accepted his religious calling: prophet, visionary, warrior, leader, peacemaker, and political mediator.

HOW DID ISLAM BEGIN?

Islam began when Muhammad came to trust that the experiences he had in the cave near Mecca really were from God and that he wasn't mentally ill or under the influence of a demon (or "jinn," as they were called in his culture). In sociological terms, Muhammad didn't simply found a new religion; he founded a new tribe inside Bedouin culture, which centered on worship of the one true God, or "Allah" (which is simply the Arabic equivalent of the English word "god"). Bedouin culture was polytheistic, meaning that it had many gods, and each tribe had their own traditional gods.

Muhammad came to believe that the primary deity of his tribe was one and the same as the deity of Judaism and Christianity and was the only true God. The term "Islam" derives from the Arabic root words which mean both "peace" and "surrender." So, to be a Muslim is to surrender to the one God and to experience the peace that comes from that surrender.

In creating a new religion and tribe oriented around worship of this one true God, Muhammad had to effectively do for his tribe what other Bedouin tribal leaders had to do for their own: keep the people safe, provide for their needs, make sure the routes between the oases in the desert were open to them, ally with other tribes for mutual benefit, administer justice and mediate disputes, and sometimes even fight militarily to fend off threats and attacks. Within 100 years of Muhammad's death, Islam had grown beyond its Bedouin roots and was on its way to becoming a world religion.

TELL ME MORE ABOUT MUHAMMAD'S WIFE, KHADIJA—DID SHE SUPPORT HER HUSBAND'S WORK AS A PROPHET?

Yes, and she is revered by Muslims everywhere for her unfailing love and support for her husband, especially after he began having the spiritual experiences in the cave near Mecca that changed his life (and hers) forever. During the first of these experiences, tradition says the angel Gabriel appeared as the mouthpiece of God, spoke to Muhammad, and commanded him to recite back what he heard. He rushed home shaken and afraid to tell Khadija what had happened. The tradition holds that she held him, calmed him, and told him to wait and see if he had the experience again.

When the experience repeated itself, she and Muhammad's other close associates supported him, helped him determine that these were legitimate experiences, and encouraged him to do what God was asking him to do. During his two decades of work as a prophet and leader, Khadija supported her husband and stood with him as he was challenged and attacked. Although Bedouin culture allowed plural marriage for men, Muhammad didn't take another wife until after Khadija died. She and their youngest daughter, Fatima, are two of the most respected women in Islam.

WHERE IS MECCA?

Mecca is near the western side of Saudi Arabia, about halfway up the coast along the Red Sea. Muhammad was born there in about 570 CE, when it was a prominent trading city. He lived there for many years, including the years when he had his spiritual experiences and founded Islam. For this reason, Mecca is the holiest city in Islam, and Muslims position themselves to face Mecca during their daily prayers.

Medina, also in Saudi Arabia, is a second holy city a few hundred miles to the northeast of Mecca, where Muhammad and his followers moved in 622 CE to escape persecution and pressure from various groups in Mecca. Muhammad set up what is thought of as the first Muslim government there, and he is buried there.

A third holy city is Jerusalem, in modern-day Israel, where Muslims built a mosque in 692 CE called the Dome of the Rock. The site is the same as the ancient Jewish temple, which was destroyed by the Romans in 70 CE. Muslims believe the site is where Abraham offered to sacrifice his son Ishmael and also where Muhammed ascended into heaven and had his role as prophet affirmed by God and all the prophets who had gone before him.

IS THE ONE GOD OF ISLAM THE SAME AS THE DEITY IN JUDAISM AND CHRISTIANITY?

According to commonly held Muslim belief, Allah and God are the same in all three religions. In general, Jews and Christians accept that Muslims worship the same deity as they do. That said, representatives from each of the three faiths may disagree on the issue due to significant differences in belief.

Islamic tradition tells its own versions of many of the events first narrated in the Hebrew scriptures, including God's encounters with other important figures like Abraham, Moses, and others. Additionally, Islam does not affirm the divinity of Jesus as Christians do. For Islam, Jesus is another prophet of God—to be respected, certainly, but not divine. Nor does Islam affirm the Holy Spirit as divine. For Muslims, the doctrine of the Trinity in Christianity—one God expressed in three persons—compromises the oneness of God.

DO MUSLIMS HAVE DIETARY CODES LIKE JEWS DO?

Yes, although the Muslim dietary codes are not as complex, overall, as the codes in Judaism. The Jewish codes, which are called kosher (see "Everyday Judaism: Keeping Kosher," page 33), lay out what foods can and cannot be eaten and how they can and cannot be prepared or served. Kosher codes forbid certain foods outright, such as pork and shellfish, and also forbid the mixing of meat and dairy. Observant Jews who keep the kosher codes will store milk and dairy products in different refrigerators and cook and serve them in separate cookware and tableware. The Islamic dietary codes—called *halal*—are not as all-encompassing. Halal codes mostly apply to meat and how the animals are to be raised and slaughtered for meat.

Everyday Islam

Keeping Halal

Muslims around the world observe halal dietary codes every day. Under this code, some foods are considered halal, which is usually translated as "permitted" or "lawful." The opposite of halal is *haram*—"not lawful" or "not permitted." Halal and haram primarily refer to meat, although any food substance not fit for consumption may be considered haram.

The two foods uniformly considered haram are pork and alcohol; however, in order for meat from domestic animals to be deemed halal, the animals must be reared and slaughtered in a certain way. The animal must be raised humanely, and, at the time of slaughter, those killing the animal must offer thanks to God, ensure the head of the animal is facing Mecca, and kill it with a single cut to the jugular. The animal's carcass must then be drained of all blood. Many consider halal meat healthier than meat from animals raised in factory farms, mainly because halal animals have lived in better conditions and been fed healthier foods.

WHAT ARE THE MAIN BELIEFS AND PRACTICES OF ISLAM?

The Five Pillars are the most common summary of the core beliefs and practices of Islam, across all its major groups and divisions. They are as follows:

1. **The confession of faith:** *"There is no God but God, and Muhammad is His Prophet."* Anyone who says this and believes it is a Muslim.

2. **Prayer:** Ritual prayer is offered five times a day (three times a day for some Shi'ite groups) at specific times. Muslims pray, wherever they are, facing Mecca, after they perform ritual washing (see "Everyday Islam: The Call to Prayer," page 137).

3. **Almsgiving:** About 2 percent, or 1/40th, of one's income is to be given to support the poor and to support the faith. In Muslim countries, this may be paid as a formal tax.

4. **Fasting:** All healthy adult Muslims are required to fast during the month of Ramadan, the month in which Muhammad first began to receive revelations in the cave. Each day for an entire month, from sunrise to sunset, observant Muslims refrain from all food, drink, and sexual relations. Those who are ill, pregnant, or otherwise unable to fast may be exempted or can observe it at a different time of year.

5. **Pilgrimage:** All Muslims whose health and finances allow it are expected to journey to Mecca at least once and undergo the annual pilgrimage, which includes various ritual actions and reenactments of

stories of Abraham, Ishmael and his mother, Hagar, and Muhammad. Portions of the alms collected by mosques and other religious organizations may go to help people who could not otherwise afford the pilgrimage.

In addition to these Five Pillars, Islam affirms ethical and moral values that would be familiar to nearly everyone from any other religious tradition, including prohibitions against lying, stealing, murder, sexual immorality, and other negative and harmful behaviors. Islam also affirms the cultivation of classic virtues like humility, honesty, integrity, piety, and other positive qualities.

WHAT KIND OF SACRED SPACES DO MUSLIMS BUILD?

The most recognizable sacred space in Islam is the mosque. A mosque can be small or large, ornate or plain, depending on when and where it was built and what particular group of Muslims it serves. Many mosques serve all Muslims—Sunni, Shi'ite, and Sufi. Others are more distinctly geared toward one group or another.

A classic feature of most mosques is their tall, slender towers called minarets, from which the mosque leaders sing or chant the daily calls to prayer. Another distinct feature of Islamic architecture and art in the mosque is that there will be no figural artwork—no statues, paintings, or drawings of God, Muhammad, or any other person. Islamic art is dominated by three primary elements: geometric designs, Arabic calligraphy, and repeating vegetal patterns (like strands of ivy or flowers) that are sometimes called "arabesque" in interior design communities. Many mosques are adorned with complex and intricate patterns containing one or all of these primary elements.

In general, mosque interiors have large, open spaces with patterns on the floor rugs that make it easy for large numbers of people to line up for prayers. In most mosques, men and women are assigned different sections; typically, women are in the back so that their modesty can be maintained while they perform the ritual movements during the prayers.

WHAT DOES THE CRESCENT AND STAR SYMBOLIZE?

The crescent and star (page 120) is the most recognizable symbol of Islam, despite the fact that it isn't really the official symbol of the religion. Instead, it was adopted by the Ottomans when their empire took Constantinople. Some evidence suggests that the crescent and star was the symbol of the city that predated the Ottoman takeover and that the Ottomans adopted the symbol as a way to maintain a transition in rule. Regardless, the Ottomans had thoroughly transformed the symbol by the later part of the 18th century. Many other Muslim groups and predominantly Muslim countries have taken on the symbol as part of their own Islamic identity, which further solidifies the symbol in Islam. It appears on the national flags of many of these countries.

WHAT ARE THE SACRED TEXTS IN ISLAM?

The primary sacred text in Islam is the *Quran*. It was compiled in the 7th century CE, not long after Muhammad died, and is considered to be the literal words of God in Arabic. Because of this understanding, Islam has never emphasized the translation of the *Quran* into other languages. All Muslims everywhere, regardless of their native languages, are expected to learn enough Arabic to say some daily prayers in Arabic and to read certain passages from the *Quran* in its original language.

A key secondary text in Islam is called the *Hadith*, or the "traditions" of the prophet. This *Hadith* is a collection of stories from the life of Muhammad, who is viewed as the ideal Muslim and a role model for all others. Each story is accompanied by a list of names, which serve to validate the reliability of the story; this list points to a lineage of people who knew Muhammad personally, were present when the events of the story occurred, or passed it down to colleagues who eventually wrote it down and collected it into the *Hadith* volume.

This concern for accuracy and reliability is a common thread across all of Islam with regard to its sacred texts. Islam has general reverence for the people and religions of Judaism and Christianity; however, according to Islamic belief, the sacred texts of those two religions lost their integrity over the centuries. No one knows for certain who wrote them, and there were long periods of oral transmission and conflicting textual traditions. By contrast, the *Quran*, in the Islamic view, is a text that was compiled during the lifetime of Muhammad, and the record of its compilation (as well as that of the *Hadith*) is much more well-known and verified than either the Jewish or Christian scriptures.

WHO WROTE THE *QURAN*?

The term "quran" means "recitation," which refers to God's revelations to Muhammad in the cave. In each episode, according to the tradition, he was asked to "recite back" to God what had been revealed. Muhammad experienced these revelatory episodes for over 20 years and recited their content to his close associates, as well as to the community at large, who stored them in their memory and shared them with others in the community. Ostensibly, some began writing down the memorized recitations, perhaps even during Muhammad's lifetime.

The caliphs, who led the Muslim community after Muhammed's death, began the process of committing to writing all the content Muhammad had revealed to people and gathering all the pieces that had already been written down. Initial collections of the *Quran,* which is a compilation of those recitations, were completed under the leadership of Abu Bakr, the first caliph. A more definitive version was completed under Uthman, the third caliph to lead after Muhammad. A few other variations emerged, but they differed mainly in the arrangement of content.

Overall, the *Quran* as a text was "completed" within a few decades of Muhammad's death. Many Muslims worldwide, however, have known of the *Quran*'s contents not by reading it but by hearing it spoken or chanted from memory by leaders in their communities. So, despite its textual integrity, the *Quran* has had long periods of oral transmission.

WHY DO WOMEN IN ISLAM SOMETIMES COVER THEIR HAIR OR FACE?

It was common practice in Bedouin culture, as well as in Jewish and Christian cultures at the time of Muhammad and beyond, for women to wear head coverings. In general, Muslim women wear head coverings for the same reasons their Jewish and Christian counterparts wear them: to preserve their modesty.

Muslim tradition on this varies according to the history and culture of a given place. Women in Iran, for example, may wear Western clothes, like jeans or pants suits, along with a scarf to cover their hair, while Saudi Arabian women cover not only their hair but their entire bodies in a cloak-like garment called the *abaya*. Some Indian Muslims will cover their heads but leave some of their hair showing, while other Muslim women from Iraq, Turkey, or the Palestinian territories will make sure that no hair shows from under their coverings. Some areas under the cultural influence of the most conservative forms of Islam—for example, in Afghanistan—require that women cover their entire faces and bodies in something like a *burka*. In short, the traditions vary depending on the place.

In general, Islam encourages modest dress for both women and men (Muslim men rarely wear short pants

Everyday Islam

The Call to Prayer

Regular prayer is one of the Five Pillars of Islam (see page 131). The traditional practice is to pray facing Mecca, usually on a prayer rug, after having washed one's hands, feet, nose, ears, and mouth. Most mosques have outdoor fountains where believers can perform their washing. But mosques aren't necessary for daily prayer; Muslims can pray anywhere.

Observant Sunni Muslims pray five times a day at specified times, and they pray according to a standard script while performing prescribed movements (i.e., standing, bowing, kneeling, and touching one's forehead to the ground). Some Shi'ite groups condense the prayer times to three times a day.

In countries or neighborhoods with a Muslim majority, the call to prayer at the specified times may be broadcast via amplification or loudspeaker from the mosque so that all Muslims in the vicinity may hear that it's time to pray.

or go without shirts). Specifically, a woman's hair is seen to be part of her sexuality and should be kept hidden from all but her close family members and her husband.

HOW DID ISLAM SPREAD?

Islam has spread through conversion, natural increase, and empire. Even during Muhammad's lifetime, the Muslim community had to fight to defend itself against pressure and persecution. One way of ensuring safety and freedom of worship for the community was to politically take over an area. In this way, Islam became associated with political power early in its history. The first Muslim political dynasty—the Umayyad dynasty, centered in Damascus and later in Spain—began only three decades after Muhammad's death.

Many other Islamic dynasties and empires followed and were central to the spread of the faith into all parts of the world. In many of these empires, conversion to Islam was not required by those who were taken over; their conversions to Islam came later, on a voluntary basis, or through natural cultural assimilation. Additionally, wandering Sufi mystics spread the faith into parts of Africa and beyond, similar to how Buddhist monks brought Buddhism into parts of central Asia.

I'VE HEARD THAT ISLAM SPREAD THROUGH "HOLY WAR" OR JIHAD—IS THAT TRUE?

Not exactly. "Jihad" is a term you may have learned through world news, but it has a distinct and different meaning in traditional Islam.

Islam spread into many parts of the world through empire or dynasty, much in the same way that Christianity came to England with William the Conqueror in 1066 CE. Empires and dynasties have armies and weapons, so to the extent that the faith is part of the political empire being fought for and established, the faiths of these empires and dynasties spread, at least in part, by "the sword."

That said, "holy war" is a term first used by Christians during the Crusades of the 10th to 13th centuries, when they went to war with Muslims for political possession of Jerusalem and the surrounding holy lands. The Arabic term "jihad" means "struggle" and, for Islam, is usually seen as having both armed and unarmed aspects to it. Armed jihad—or jihad of the sword—is an armed struggle to defend Muslims and others in their rights to worship and practice their faiths. Jihad of the heart or spirit is the unarmed struggle to live a virtuous life of submission to God.

WHAT ARE THE MAIN GROUPS WITHIN ISLAM?

The two major divisions within Islam are the Sunni and Shi'ite. Eighty-five percent of the world's Muslims are Sunni; Shi'ites comprise the remaining 15 percent. The division between these two groups traces back to the time of Muhammad and has to do primarily with differing views regarding who was to succeed him in leadership.

The Sunni—which means "of the tradition" or "of the community"—believed that the community should be led by someone they believed held close to the teachings and traditions of Muhammad. They chose Abu Bakr. The Shi'ites—"shia" means "party of" or "group of"—felt that a blood relative should succeed Muhammad, so they chose Ali (Muhammad's cousin and son-in-law) from among his close associates, becoming the "party of Ali." Sunni and Shi'ite Muslims, therefore, trace different lineages of leadership back to the time of the prophet and, thus, have developed different lines of authority and theology over the centuries. There are further subgroups within both Sunni and Shi'ite Islam. Sufis, another group within Islam, may be either Sunni or Shi'ite in their orientation, but they focus on the mystical wisdom traditions of Islam.

OTHER THAN MUHAMMAD, WHO ARE THE MOST IMPORTANT PEOPLE IN ISLAM?

The four caliphs, who were Muhammad's close associates, were very important for early Islam's development and spread. After them, the leaders of various dynasties and empires, including the leaders of the Umayyads, Mongols, Mughals, and Ottomans. Additionally, Islam has a number of philosophers and scholars who were highly influential during the medieval period in the West—men like Ibn Sina, Ibn Rushd, and al-Ghazali. Finally, there is Rumi, the 13th-century jurist and writer who has become one of the most famous poets in the world.

DOES ISLAM REVERE JESUS AND ALL THE PROPHETS AND LEADERS FROM JUDAISM?

Yes, in general. Islam sees itself as continuing a prophetic tradition, centered around the one God, that began with the ancient Israelites and continued through the life of

Jesus and the founding of Christianity. Islam honors all the Jewish prophets and leaders of the Hebrew Bible, as well as Jesus from the Christian tradition. Many of the stories found in the Jewish and Christian scriptures are also found, with distinctly Islamic variations, in the *Quran*. For example, the *Quran* includes references to Adam, Noah, Abraham, and many other figures from both the Jewish and Christian texts, as well as stories about Jesus' birth and his mother, Mary.

As mentioned earlier, Islam does not revere Jesus as a divine being, as this would compromise the oneness of God. Additionally, Islam does not teach that Jesus died via crucifixion. In the Islamic view, God would not allow his prophet to undergo such a humiliating death; therefore, Jesus ascended into heaven prior to his suffering on the cross, and, via divine fiat, another person (a disciple, perhaps—Islamic scholars differ on this and the *Quran* isn't definitive) was miraculously transformed to look like Jesus and died on the cross in his stead.

WHAT DOES ISLAM TEACH ABOUT THE AFTERLIFE?

Islam and Christianity have similar views of the afterlife. Islam teaches the existence of heaven and hell, which are places of eternal reward and punishment. Muslims believe that when they die, their souls remain in their graves until the Day of Judgment at the end of time, during which everyone will be judged for their deeds and beliefs. Based on that judgment from God and his angels, people will spend eternity in either heaven or hell. Before the Day of Judgment, Jesus—or "Isa," as he is called in the *Quran*—will return to earth to fight a false messiah who is very similar to what Christianity calls the Antichrist. A dominant branch of Shi'ite Islam teaches that the 12th imam in their lineage of leaders after Muhammad underwent a spiritual occultation and exists in hidden form among their communities. This hidden imam is known as the "Mahdi" or "rightly guided one." According to those who believe in him, he will reveal himself in the last days in a return of sorts and, alongside Jesus, will fight the Antichrist to destroy evil in the world.

I'VE HEARD OF THE POET RUMI—WAS HE MUSLIM?

Yes, Rumi was a Muslim who was born in what is now Afghanistan in the 13th century CE. His father was an esteemed Muslim scholar and raised Rumi to follow in his footsteps. Rumi moved with his family to Mecca, then to Aleppo and Damascus after his father died. There, he studied Islamic law and was initiated into Sufism.

He moved to Konya, Turkey, in 1240 and there, a few years later, began what became a profound spiritual relationship with a wandering mystic named Shams al-Din from Tabriz. Rumi's relationship with Shams was all-consuming, and Rumi turned away from being the renowned Muslim intellectual and jurist he'd been up to that point. After Sham's death in 1247, Rumi began to write the dazzling love poetry that he is famous for today. For many people in the West, Rumi is their first exposure to Sufi mysticism. His work has entered into pop culture through artists like Madonna and others, although its Islamic aspects are often minimized.

How Islam Relates to Other Major Religions

Islam is a highly influential religion, second in size only to Christianity. Between the two of them, they contain over half of all religiously affiliated people in the world. Judaism is the parent religion to both of them, and Islam mirrors both Christianity and Judaism in many of its core beliefs.

- Jews, Christians, and Muslims are called "people of the book," in reference to the high reverence believers show toward the shared textual narratives and stories that permeate all three religions and their sacred texts.

- Like other religions that have entangled themselves with empires or dynasties (i.e., Buddhism, Christianity, or Taoism), Islam's history includes periods of intolerance as well as of peaceful coexistence with peoples of other faiths.

- Islam joins Catholicism, Protestantism, Buddhism, and Taoism as one of five officially recognized religions in China. The government manages the leadership of these religions and, in the case of official Islam, aids the observant in going on pilgrimage. Other groups of Muslims, like the Uighurs, as well as unofficial groups of and other religions, are not supported and are sometimes persecuted.

- Judaism, Islam, and Sikhism are staunchly iconoclastic with regard to statues depicting the God or any prophets, sages, or gurus. Sikhism allows paintings of the gurus, much like some forms of Protestant Christianity allow paintings of Jesus and his disciples.

THE KHANDA, PAGE 159

CHAPTER SEVEN

Sikhism

Sikhism is a 500-plus-year-old religion that began in the Punjab region of northern India. The religion began in both a Hindu and Muslim context, so Sikhism contains influences from both of these religions, as well as from a devotional movement called the Sant tradition that developed in India a few generations prior to Sikhism's founding. In many ways, Sikhism is very simple; it is a strong monotheism that exhorts people to live virtuously, serve others, and develop increasing "God consciousness" in their lives.

Despite having existed for only a few hundred years, Sikhism has spread throughout the world, especially in areas connected to the British Empire. Sikhism is a fascinating case study in how religions are organic, dynamic systems that change over time in order to stay relevant. As you'll read in this chapter, Sikhism has undergone significant organizational and structural changes in its short history, which only serve to make this religion even more interesting and engaging.

Cheat Sheet

When it began: around 1500 CE

Number of adherents: about 25 million

Percentage of world population: less than 1 percent

Primary location: 90 percent of Sikhs live in northern India; there are also concentrations of Sikhs in the United Kingdom, the United States, and Canada

Largest sect/denomination: no official denominations or sects; the Khalsa and the Sahajdaris are the two major groups of Sikhs

Primary text: the *Adi Granth* (also called the Guru Granth Sahib)

Most recognizable symbol: the khanda (page 144), as well as a pictorial image of Guru Nanak and the nine gurus who succeeded him

KEY DATES

1200s CE	The Sant Mat Movement, a devotional mystical movement in India focused on the lives of saintly people in Hinduism, provides much of the spiritual and cultural context for the ethos of Sikshim.
1469–1539	The founder of Sikhism, Nanak, lives.
1459–1534	Bhai Mardana lives. He was Guru Nanak's longtime Muslim companion and first convert to Sikhism.
1581–1606	Leadership of Arjan, the fifth guru.
1604	Construction of the Golden Temple, the sacred space of Sikhism.
1603–1604	Compilation of the *Adi Granth*.
1675–1708	Leadership of Gobind Singh, the tenth and last guru.
1699	Establishment of the new Sikh order, the Khalsa.
1780–1839	Ranjit Singh, the "Lion of the Punjab," founder and ruler of a Sikh kingdom in northern India from 1801 to 1839, lives.
1845–1849	Anglo-Sikh Wars: conflict between the British and the Sikh kingdom for control of northern India.
1920–1925	The Gurdwara Reform Movement occurs—a nonviolent campaign to transfer control of Sikh places of worship away from those it had been handed over to during 18th-century Mughal rule.
1984	Indian Prime Minister Indira Gandhi assassinated by Sikh bodyguards in the wake of her Operation Blue Star, which sought to quell Sikh nationalism.

On the Sikh Calendar

Sikhs celebrate several of the main Hindu festivals, modifying them to their own beliefs and narratives. They also mark their own distinct celebrations, most of which revolve around the lives of the 10 gurus.

VAISAKHI

April 13 or 14

Vaisakhi, the Sikh New Year, commemorates the founding of the Khalsa. Sikh flags are replaced with new ones, and people gather for continuous readings of the entire text of the sacred *Adi Granth*.

DIWALI

October or November

An autumn festival of lights (also celebrated by Hindus) that lasts for four to five days. For Sikhs, it commemorates the freeing of the sixth guru from prison. People decorate their homes and *gurdwaras* (community centers or sacred spaces) with lights.

GURPURBS

Date varies

These are the many annual Sikh celebrations that commemorate the births and deaths of the 10 gurus who led the religion in its beginnings. Special attention is given to those gurus who were killed or martyred, like Arjan (fifth guru) and Bahadur (ninth guru). People gather for public competitions and processions and meet up in the gurdwara for special communal meals and readings of the *Adi Granth*.

Burning Questions

WHO STARTED SIKHISM?

Sikhism was started by Nanak, who lived in the Punjab region of northern India in the late 15th and early 16th centuries. He was raised in a Hindu family but was also comfortable in the Muslim culture present in that part of India at the time. When he was about 30 years old, he had a spiritual experience that altered the trajectory of his life. While engaging in regular morning devotionals and bathing at a nearby river with his friends, he disappeared. His friends dragged the river to find him, thinking he had drowned, but found nothing. Three days later, Nanak reappeared and claimed that he'd been taken up into the presence of God, who revealed to him as the "True Name." He was given nectar to drink and was commissioned to spread the message of the one God, who is neither Hindu nor Muslim but beyond all such irrelevant distinctions.

Nanak embarked on a journey around India with his musician Muslim friend, Mardana, to share a message of devotion to the one God. After about 20 years, Nanak returned to his home in the Punjab, bringing disciples with him and establishing the first Sikh community. Before he died, he appointed Angad—one of his followers, rather than one of his sons as was a custom—to be the next guru, or "teacher."

WHY IS THE RELIGION CALLED "SIKHISM"? WHAT IS "SIKH"?

The religion's name derives from the word "sikkha" in the Punjabi language, which means "disciple" and "to learn." The term was first used in Sikh history for the people who listened to the message of Nanak and Mardana as they traveled around India, exhorting devotion to the one God revealed to Nanak in his religious experience. Later, many of those followers came with him back to the Punjab region to establish the first Sikh community of disciples and learners.

WHAT IS A GURU?

A guru in the Sikh (and Hindu) context is a teacher, specifically a personal teacher who directs one's spiritual growth. Usually, students learn directly from their gurus—sitting at their feet or in small groups or audiences—and gurus have some form of a personal relationship with their students. In short, their students aren't simply anonymous people in a crowd; gurus know their students personally to some extent and are, thus, able to give them somewhat customized spiritual guidance, alongside their general teachings. Nanak became known as a guru as he traveled around India and taught those who responded to his message. Many of these disciples joined him as he returned to his hometown.

OTHER THAN NANAK, WHO ARE THE MOST IMPORTANT PEOPLE IN SIKHISM?

The nine gurus who followed Nanak are the most important people in Sikhism. Most Sikh holidays are centered around the lives of the gurus—their birthdays, or the days when they died. Many of the most notable achievements in the development of the religion were accomplished by one or more of the nine gurus. The sacred text of Sikhism contains several thousand hymns, poems, and other writings from the first five gurus (including Nanak), as well as from saintly figures from Hinduism and Islam whose ideas cohere with Sikh spirituality, making them important figures as well. Additionally, anyone whose words appear in the *Adi Granth*, which is the primary sacred text in Sikhism, are also important.

TELL ME MORE ABOUT THE SCRIPTURE OF SIKHISM—WHO WROTE IT?

The primary text of Sikhism is the *Adi Granth* ("first book"), which is also usually referred to as the "living guru." The text was compiled in 1603 and 1604 under the leadership of the Arjan, the fifth guru. It contains writings and hymns from the first five gurus, including Nanak, Kabir (a 14th-century poet from the Sant devotional movement in India), and a variety of Hindu and Muslim saints and mystics whose ideas resonate with those of Nanak and Sikhism in general.

The text as the "living guru" became the focus of Sikhism after the 10th guru changed the leadership structure of the religion. In Sikhism's new structure, the text itself, rather than a human guru, became authoritative and central as the teacher of the Sikh community. The text lives eternally, unlike human gurus; thus, it is the eternally "living guru." As such, the *Adi Granth* is treated with the same respect a human guru might receive. It is housed in a special closet or space, it is carried via processional into the communal rooms of the gurdwara or people's homes, and it is placed on a special stand. It is fanned as people are reading from it, and it is carried back to its space to be "put to bed," draped with special cloths and other adornments when the readings are completed.

WHY DON'T OBSERVANT SIKHS CUT THEIR HAIR?

One of the traits or markers of men and women who have been initiated into the Khalsa is that they do not cut their hair. In the Indian Hindu context, refraining from cutting one's hair is part of the process of ascetic renunciation of regular, everyday, householder life. One stops paying attention to physical appearances and gives all of one's energies to spiritual effort. Sikhism takes a slightly different approach; refraining from cutting hair is simply one of the five primary actions or adornments that mark a person as having made a deep commitment to Sikhism and to defending the faith. Sikhs who don't cut their hair are not renouncers at all; they continue in their everyday lives. Unlike Hindu renouncers (sannyasi), whose hair is often unkempt, Sikhs keep theirs neat.

WHAT IS THE KHALSA?

The Khalsa, which means "pure," is a committed community of soldier-saints. It is a community of the pure, initially set up by Gobind Singh, the ninth guru, when he transitioned the leadership of the entire religion away from a human guru and toward the sacred text and community. Initially, the Khalsa had a political and militaristic impulse, geared toward defending the Sikh community from pressure and persecution under the Muslim Mughal Empire in India. Part of that impulse remains today, but, for most Sikhs, the Khalsa is more of a spiritual community than a political or militaristic one.

Initiation into the Khalsa—one of only a handful of rituals that Sikhism maintains—indicates the most serious level of commitment to the tenets of the religion and to the community. People mark that commitment through five external features: uncut hair (*kes*), a comb (*kangha*), a sword (*kirpan*), a steel bracelet (*kara*), and long shorts (*kachha*). These are sometimes called the Five Ks of the Khalsa, since they all start with the Punjabi sound that is the letter "k" in English.

SO, SIKHS IN THE KHALSA REALLY CARRY SWORDS?

Yes, but not necessarily a long, full-size sword that fits in a scabbard on a belt. Some Sikhs might wear one of these as part of a special ceremony, holiday, or similar occasion. Most Sikhs, however, carry smaller swords or knives that look like small swords. Or, they may not carry an actual sword or knife at all. Instead, they may wear a small sword emblem on a necklace, sort of like how some Christians wear a small cross on a necklace. Some Sikhs may carry a small sword-shaped trinket in their pocket, purse, or wallet. The point is that the sword is a marker that signifies the wearer's commitment to their faith and to God to the Sikh who wears or carries it, as well as to anyone else who may see it and knows what it means.

WHAT DO MOST SIKHS DO AS A MAIN FORM OF WORSHIP OR PRACTICE?

Observant Sikhs participate in daily devotionals at home that involve singing, chanting, meditation, and scripture reading. They will also gather regularly, usually weekly, at the local gurdwara with other Sikhs and their guests for scripture readings, teachings, singing, and to share the *langar*, or the communal meal.

Sikhs practice a few other notable rituals, including those associated with initiation into the Khalsa. One is baptized into the Khalsa by having sugar water that has been stirred with a sword sprinkled over one's head and eyes. Another ritual is called taking the *Hukam* ("command") and involves randomly opening the *Adi Granth* and reading the page it opens to in order to gain guidance for a certain circumstance or to choose the name of a child. Finally, another common ritual is called *Paath* ("reading"), which involves reading the entire *Adi Granth* in one sitting either continuously without breaks or over a longer multi-day period (for example, during a period of mourning after a death).

Everyday Sikhism

Communal Meal

Sikhs usually meet once a week in the gurdwara (the Sikh local meeting space) for a communal meal (langar). Often, these meals are not limited to Sikhs but are open to all. This tradition traces back to Nanak himself, who, according to Sikh stories, often intentionally shared meals with groups of people. What was distinct about these communal meals is that everyone was welcome, regardless of caste, which violated deep-seated norms in India regarding intercaste fellowship. Sikhism today still opens the communal meal and the entire religion to all. In diaspora areas (places where Sikhs live outside of northern India), Sikh communities are often known for their generosity in feeding people in need. In these instances, the communal meal takes on a dimension of community service.

Generally, however, Sikhism does not emphasize numerous or elaborate enactments of ritual, especially compared to Hinduism, which was Nanak's birth religion. This traces back to Nanak himself, who deemed most religious ritual unnecessary and even harmful to true spirituality. He and other leaders in Sikhism focus on the interiority of the religion—how one brings spiritual life into one's heart—rather than on the external performance of religion.

WHAT IS THE LARGER GOAL OF SIKH SPIRITUAL PRACTICE? WHAT ARE THEY TRYING TO ACHIEVE?

The larger spiritual goal of Sikhism is to achieve *mukti*, or "spiritual liberation," from the cycle of life, death, and rebirth. Like Hinduism, Sikhism affirms this cycle and the karma that propels it forward indefinitely until one is liberated from it. All Sikh practices and teachings from scripture—the devotional effort, singing, chanting, meditating, serving the community, cultivating virtues, and eliminating vice—are designed to increase God-consciousness and aid the transition from being a *manmukh* (a spiritually degenerated person) to a *gurmukh* (a regenerated person). A manmukh lives a life of lust, anger, pride, covetousness, and attachment to worldly goods.

Through spiritual effort, a person can regenerate themself and live a life of truth, compassion, patience, contentment, and service to God and others, and they can achieve mukti in this life and in the afterlife. This resonates with much of Hinduism and Islamic Sufism (mysticism). However, the Sikh distinction is that this process of spiritual regeneration is to begin as a child and continue throughout one's life, as one goes about living everyday life. One does not have to become a monk or a nun or a renouncer alone in the forest.

WHAT KIND OF SACRED SPACE DOES SIKHISM HAVE?

The gurdwara is the most basic sacred space, although it's mostly a community center. It may or may not be highly adorned. In fact, most gurdwaras look and feel like a community center, with the exception of a special altar or stand for the *Adi Granth* when it is carried in via procession for readings or teachings. Most gurdwaras have large rooms for group gatherings, as well as a kitchen for preparation of the langars, the communal meals that are shared regularly between Sikhs and their guests.

The primary sacred space of global Sikhism is the Golden Temple at Amritsar in northern India; Sikhs call it *Harmandir Sahib* ("temple of God") or *Darbar Sahib* ("court of God"). This magnificent, richly gilded temple was built during the leadership of Arjan, the fifth guru, and is one of the most striking sacred spaces in the world. It is surrounded by water and is open on all four sides to symbolize that everyone—from the four official castes in Hinduism, from the four cardinal directions, from everywhere—is welcome.

WHY ARE SO MANY SIKH NAMES "SINGH" OR "KAUR"?

Traditionally, once Sikhs are initiated into the Khalsa, they take new names. Men take the name "Singh," which means "lion," and women take the name "Kaur," which means "princess" or "lioness." Over time, these names have been passed down as family names to people who aren't part of the Khalsa or even the Sikh community. In recent years, especially among Sikhs living outside of India, the tradition of taking a new name has become less common than in past generations. Many Sikhs now, upon entering the Khalsa, keep their given names.

WHY DO SIKH MEN WEAR TURBANS?

Turbans are one of the most visible markers of Sikh men (and some women). The turban, however, is not really an official part of Sikh observance. Instead, the turban is connected to two of the Five Ks of Khalsa that have to do with members not cutting their hair and carrying a comb. Both men and women in the Khalsa refrain from cutting their hair; however, the Sikh practice is distinct from the Hindu ascetics who withdraw from the world, renounce worldly possessions and concerns, and, thus, will grow their hair without washing or combing it. Sikhs comb their hair and keep it neat and clean. Sikh women will often leave their hair loose, but Sikh men will gather their long hair into a turban. They may also gather the hair of their beards into neat rolls that they tuck over their ears and into the turban. The point of the turban—for both the men and the women who wear it—is to help keep the hair neat and tidy. Over time, the turban has become one way in which Sikhs are recognizable in public.

HOW DID SIKHISM SPREAD?

Sikhism spread through missionaries, charitable work, and the spreading influence of the British empire. Nanak himself spread his teaching throughout India and beyond during his lifetime, and many of the places he visited for prolonged periods became Sikh centers. The other nine gurus also spread Sikhism through their travels and by founding various centers for study and meditation. Some gurus, especially the ninth guru, emphasized the secular nature of many Sikh enterprises, like hospitals, schools, or kitchens, to feed the hungry. They made it clear that they were open to all people, regardless of religion or caste, and would serve people without trying to convert anyone to Sikhism. Finally, as India came under British rule, Sikhs were recruited for the British military and posted around the world as part of their service. Thus, Sikhs ended up establishing religious and community centers in many parts of the world that were new to them. Today, the largest concentrations of Sikhs outside of northern India are in the United Kingdom and Canada.

DOES SIKHISM HAVE A MAJOR SYMBOL, LIKE THE CROSS FOR CHRISTIANS?

Yes, the main symbol for Sikhism is called the "khanda," a term which refers to the double-edged sword that forms the central part of the larger symbol (page 144).

Everyday Sikhism

Daily Devotionals

Daily morning devotionals are a common practice in Sikh life. Nanak himself is a role model for this practice, which reflects the influence of both the morning prayers of Islam and the daily puja for Hindus on Sikhism. For Sikhs, this daily devotional practice happens at home and involves prayers, chanting or singing, and reading passages from the *Adi Granth*.

Specifically, the morning prayer before dawn features the "Japji," a hymn written by Nanak that appears in the opening section of the *Adi Granth*. Two other hymns are featured in prayers during the rest of the day. Sikhs are encouraged to keep the teachings of the gurus, as well as the "living guru," their sacred text, on their minds and hearts throughout the day; they are also encouraged to increase their God-consciousness and live a life of virtue.

The Sikh khanda is made up of the upright two-edged sword (khanda), which is encircled by two daggers (kirpan), with a circle in the middle. The double-edged sword represents Truth or Divine Knowledge; the two daggers represent two primary forms of authority, spiritual and temporal; and the circle represents the one eternal and perfect God. Together, the elements of the symbol speak to Sikhism's core beliefs: one God, reverence for Truth, awareness of both spiritual and earthly authorities, and responsibility toward both realms of one's life.

WHAT ARE THE MAIN GROUPS WITHIN SIKHISM?

Sikhism doesn't have official denominations, like Christianity or Islam. However, there are divisions within the religion as a whole, as well as within the Khalsa. Some of these divisions can be traced back to an 18th-century reform movement in Sikhism that tried to distinguish clearly between Sikh religion and Hinduism. That reform movement defined Sikhism mostly in terms of the Khalsa and, thus, conceived of the religion in more militaristic terms.

However, this did not resonate for everyone in Sikhism, nor did they want to take upon themselves the commitments and markers of the Khalsa (i.e., the Five Ks). These Sikhs (called *Sahadjaris*, or "slow adopters," by the Khalsa members) don't cut their hair, wear the bracelet, or carry swords, and they prefer the pacifist tone set by Nanak and later gurus in the early years of the religion.

Additionally, there are divisions between tradition-alists and innovators across the religion and within the Khalsa itself. Innovators are often (although not always) found in diaspora communities outside of India that are removed, sometimes by generations, from the tradi-tional culture of Sikhism. Innovators may develop new ways to use the gurdwara space or new traditions at the langar, and traditionalists will resist these innovations. However, none of these divisions have resulted in signif-icant ruptures across Sikhism that would resemble the Protestant Reformation for Christianity, for example, or the division between Sunni and Shi'ite in Islam.

DO SIKHS WORSHIP A GOD? OR MANY GODS? OR NO GOD?

Sikhism is staunchly monotheistic and steadfastly affirms that there is but one God, or one divine reality. Moreover, Sikhism insists that the names given to God by Islam, Hinduism, and other religions are all simply human, finite iterations that attempt to define an ulti-mately ineffable reality. So, Sikhism is happy to use all the names for God common in other religions, with the understanding that all these names point to a larger, infinite divine reality than can ever be truly captured in language. Sikh meditation practices often involve chanting the divine name that Sikh's prefer, *Ik Onkar*, which is a word made up of sounds that are similar to the "om" sound chanted by Hindus, Jains, Buddhists, and others. So, again, the point is not the exact name but something more primal and infinite—a cosmic or universal sound that, when chanted, helps heighten consciousness of the divine reality.

YOU SAY SIKHISM HAS BOTH HINDU AND MUSLIM INFLUENCES—HOW SO?

Nanak was raised in a Hindu family but in a region with a strong Islamic influence. So, his own religious sensibility makes room for both of these religious traditions. Like Hinduism, Sikhism affirms the doctrine of karma and the notion that life is cyclical—involving birth, death, and rebirth—until one achieves liberation from the cycle through spiritual practice. Like Islam, Sikhism is steadfastly monotheistic and prohibits figural imagery of the divine reality. Finally, Sikhism resonates strongly with the mystical, devotional aspects of both Hinduism and Islam. In fact, the writings of several Hindu and Muslim saints known for their devotion and spiritual knowledge are featured in the sacred scriptures of the Sikh religion.

How Sikhism Relates to Other Major Religions

Sikhism, in many ways, is a simple tradition that focuses on daily spiritual practice, worship of God, and increasing God-consciousness in one's life. The religion has strong exhortations for both the individual and the community, all of which focus on developing oneself spiritually, rooting out vice, and serving the community as a whole. While Sikhism is a small religion, its influence and renown are more widespread because of its affiliation with the British Empire in the 19th and early 20th centuries.

- Sikhism shares with Hinduism, Buddhism, and Jainism a belief in karma and the larger goal of escaping the cycle of life, death, and rebirth.

- Like Islam and Judaism, Sikhism is iconoclastic: it forbids statues of the divine or of the gurus (pictures of the gurus are permitted).

- Like the Jewish community, the Sikh community has sought to have its own country or kingdom in order to secure itself against persecution on the basis of faith.

- Like the primary Abrahamic faiths (Judaism, Christianity, and Islam), Sikhism puts high emphasis on its sacred text and is sometimes included by scholars as one of the "religions of the book."

- Like Hinduism and Islam, Sikhism emphasizes daily prayer and worship at certain times of the day.

- Unlike Hinduism, Sikhism doesn't have a tradition of ascetic renunciation whereby one leaves regular householder life to devote oneself exclusively to spiritual practice. Sikhism envisions spiritual progress happening throughout all of life, through the devotional practices of everyday life.

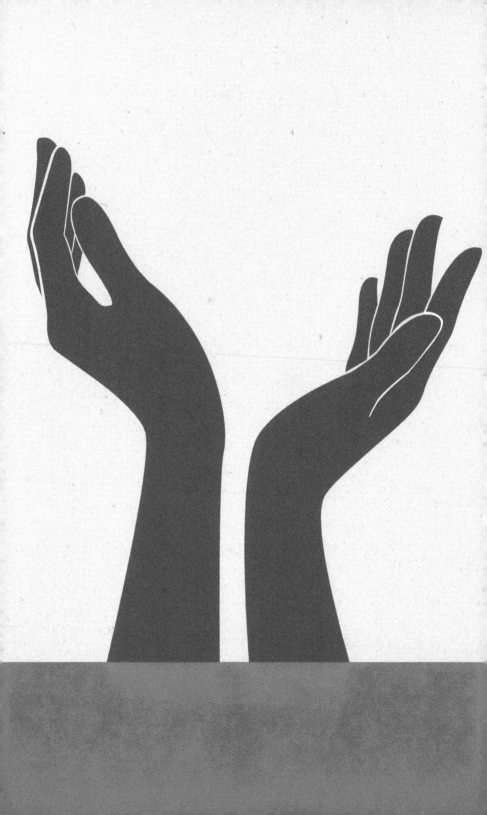

FURTHER READING

Barks, Coleman, and Michael Green. *The Illuminated Rumi.* New York: Broadway Books, 1997.

British Broadcasting Company (BBC). "Religions." BBC.co.uk/religion/religions.

Earhart, H. Byron. *Religion in Japan: Unity and Diversity.* Boston: Cengage Learning, 2013.

Hartford Institute for Religion Research, Hartford Seminary. hirr.hartsem.edu/ency.

Huyler, Stephen P. *Meeting God: Elements of Hindu Devotion.* New Haven & London: Yale University Press, 1999.

Kenyon College, Department of Religious Studies, Online Resources and Kenyon Journals. www2.Kenyon.edu/Depts/Religion/Rsrc.

My Jewish Learning. myJewishLearning.com.

Pew Research Center. "Religion and Public Life." PewForum.org.

Public Broadcasting System. "Global Connections: The Middle East." PBS.org/wgbh/globalconnections/mideast/themes/religion.

Religion News Service. ReligionNews.com.

Renard, John. *The Handy Religion Answer Book.* Detroit: Visible Ink Press, 2002.

Robinson, Thomas A., and Hillary P. Rodrigues, eds. *World Religions: A Guide to the Essentials*. Peabody, Massachusetts: Hendrickson Publishers, 2006.

Swatos, Jr., William H., ed. *Encyclopedia of Religion and Society*. Lanham, Maryland: AltaMira Press, 1998.

World Religions Professor. World-Religions -Professor.com.

REFERENCES

Biswas, Soutik. "The Myth of the Indian Vegetarian Nation." BBC News. April 4, 2018. BBC.com/news /world-asia-india-43581122.

BBC. "Religions: Parinirvana." May 7, 2004. BBC.co.uk /religion/religions/buddhism/holydays/parinirvana .shtml.

Gill, Rahuldeep Singh. "Worship and Devotion in Daily Life." Sikhism, *Patheos*. Accessed December 21, 2020. patheos.com/library/sikhism/ritual-worship -devotion-symbolism/worship-and-devotion-in -daily-life.

Hackett, Conrad, and David McClendon. "Christians Remain World's Largest Religious Group, but They Are Declining." Pew Research Center Fact Tank, News in Numbers. April 5, 2017. PewResearch.org /fact-tank/2017/04/05/christians-remain-worlds -largest-religious-group-but-they-are-declining -in-europe.

The Irish Times. "Shias Await the Return of the Twelfth Imam." August 4, 2006. IrishTimes.com/news/shias-await-the-return-of-the-twelfth-imam-1.1033888.

My Jewish Learning. "The Jewish Denominations." Accessed November 30, 2020. myJewishLearning.com/article/the-jewish-denominations.

O'Brien, Barbara. "An Overview of Bodhi Day: Commemoration of the Buddha's Enlightenment." *Learn Religions.* March 8, 2019. LearnReligions.com/bodhi-day-449913.

Pew Research Center, Religion & Public Life. "Other Religions." December 18, 2012. PewForum.org/2012/12/18/global-religious-landscape-other.

Pew Research Center, Religion & Public Life. "Buddhists." December 18, 2012. PewForum.org/2012/12/18/global-religious-landscape-buddhist.

Sikh.org. "Religious Emblems: Khanda." Accessed December 21, 2020. Sikhs.org/khanda.htm.

Williams, Jennifer. "Muslims Love Jesus, Too: 6 Things You Didn't Know about Jesus in Islam." *Vox.* Updated December 20, 2019. Vox.com/2017/12/18/10660648/jesus-in-islam-muslims-believe-christmas-quran.

INDEX

A

Abraham, 25, 37, 132
  faiths, 165
  God of, 101
  God's encounter with, 129
  Islam and, 121
  monotheisms, 68, 118
  Quran, 141
  role in Judaism, 28–29
  sacrifice of, 124, 128
  Torah and, 30
Adi Granth, Sikhism and, 20, 146, 147,
  148, 151–152, 154, 157, 160
Advent, Christian calendar 114
ahimsa (noninjury), philosophy
  of, *xiv*, 15
Ancestor Day, Buddhist calendar, 90
Apostle's Creed, 101
Aquinas, Thomas, 97
Arjan (Sikh guru), 147, 148, 151, 157
Aryans, 6
Ashoka (Emperor), 73, 78, 89
Ashvaghosha, *Buddhacarita*, 84
Ash Wednesday, Christian calendar, 114
Athanasius, 97
Atman (individual soul), Hinduism,
  7, 8, 9, 80
Augustine, 97
Avalokiteśvara
  in Buddhism, 83–84
  calendar birthday, 74

B

Baal Shem Tov, Rabbi Israel, 25
Bahadur (Sikh guru), 148
Baha'i, *xiv*
Bar mitzvah, Jewish law, 40
Bhagavad Gita, Hindu text, 2, 12
*Bible. See Catholic Bible; Christian Bible;
  Jewish Bible*
Black Hats, Taoism, 61
Bodhisattva
  Buddhist, 67, 87, 89, 90
  Mahayana school, 81, 83–84

Bodhi tree, Four Noble Truths, 77
Brahman (world soul),
  Hinduism, 7–9, 68
British East India Company, 3
British Empire, 104, 145, 159, 164
Buddha. *See also* Buddhism
  in Buddhism, 75–76
  Four Noble Truths, 77
  in Hinduism, 76–77
  on ignorant desire, 78–79
  Siddhartha Gautama, 20, 71, 73,
    75–76, 85, 87
Buddhacarita, Buddhist text, 84
Buddhism, *x*, 47
  Avalokiteśvara's birthday, 74
  Bodhi Day, 74–75
  Buddha, 20, 71, 73, 75–76, 85, 87
  calendar, 74–75
  celebrations by region, 89–90
  cheat sheet on, 72
  China and, 71, 73, 78, 82, 83
  Christianity and, 118
  connections to major religions, 92–93
  Four Noble Truths, 77
  Hinduism as parent religion, 1, 20
  Hinduism versus, 80–81
  holy of, *xii*
  India and, 71
  Islam and, 143
  karma in, 6, 79
  key dates, 73
  lotus flowers in, 90
  Mahayana, 72, 73, 80–81, 82, 83,
    89–90
  meditation, 72, 86
  monks or nuns in, 91
  Parinirvana (Nirvana Day), 74
  reincarnation, 79
  religion of, 84
  sacred sites for, 87
  schools of thought, 81, 83
  sects of, 79–80
  Sikhism and, 164
  spread of, 78

statues of happy or laughing Buddha, 85, 87
stupas, 89
Taoism and, 67
temples and sacred spaces, 88
texts, 84
Theravada, 73, 81, 89
Triple Treasure, 76
Vajrayana, 73, 83
Vesak (Buddha Day), 74
yoga and, 85
Zen, 73, 82, 83, 88
Byzantine Empire, 104, 111

C

Calvin, John, 97
Caste system, Hinduism and, 13–14
Catholic Bible, 102
Catholicism, 108, 110–111, 143
Celestial Masters school, Taoism, 62
Chan Buddhism, 73, 82
Cheat sheets
    Buddhism, 72
    Christianity, 96
    Hinduism, 2
    Islam, 122
    Judaism, 24
    Sikhism, 146
    Taoism, 48
China. See Buddhism; Islam; Taoism
Chinese New Year, Taoist calendar, 50
Christian Bible, 31, 102
Christianity, x, xi
    afterlife in, 113
    Buddhism and, 93
    calendar, 98–99
    Catholic and Protestant
        Christians, 110–111
    cheat sheet on, 96
    connections to other
        religions, 118–119
    cross or crucifix symbol,
        108, 109, 110
    deity of, 128–129
    dietary codes in, 106–107
    disciples of Jesus, 102–103
    doctrine of Trinity, 101
    "gospel" in, 115
    holidays in, 113–114
    Holy Spirit in Trinity, 115–116
    influence on world, 96
    Islam and, 143
    Jesus, 95, 100
    Jesus' death, 107–108
    Jewish scriptures and, 116
    Judaism and, 44–45, 104, 106
    key dates, 97
    meaning of "Christ", 99
    Orthodox, 98, 102, 108, 111, 112
    Paul the Apostle in, 114–115
    professional clergy, 112–113
    sacraments in, 112
    saints and angels, 116–117
    scriptures of, 102
    spread of, 103–104
    Sundays for church, 105
Christmas, Christian calendar, 98, 113
Chuang tzu Taoist master, 49, 52–53, 57, 65
    Taoist text, 48, 49, 52, 55
Confucianism, xiv, 47, 54
    Buddhism and, 93
    Taoism and, 65–66, 67
Confucius, 65
Conservative Judaism, 36, 38
Council at Nicea, 97, 101
Cows, in Hinduism, 15
Crescent and star symbol, Islam, 133
Cross symbol, Christianity, 108, 109, 110
Crucifix, Christianity, 108, 109, 110
Culture, religion and, x–xi

D

Dalai Lama, 47, 73, 84
Dao shi (Taoist priest), 59
Dao Zhang, Taoist text, 55
David (King), 25, 34, 43
Day of Atonement, Jewish calendar, 27
Deity. See Islam; Judaism; Christianity
Devi/Durga, Hindu goddess, 10

Dietary codes
Christianity, 106–107
Islamic, 129, 130
Judaism's kosher, 33
Disciples, Jesus and, 102–103
Diwali
Hindu calendar, 5
Sikh calendar, 148
Dome of the Rock, 35, 128
Dragon Boat Festival, Taoist calendar, 51
Durga Puja, Hindu calendar, 5

E

Easter, Christian calendar, 99, 113–114
Eid Al-Adha, Islamic calendar, 124
Eid Al-Fitr, Islamic calendar, 124
Epiphany, Christian calendar, 98, 114

F

Fatima, daughter of Muhammad, 127
Feast of the Sacrifice, Islamic
calendar, 124
Feast of Weeks, Jewish calendar, 26
Festival of Breaking the Fast, Islamic
calendar, 124
Festival of Color, Hindu calendar, 4
Festival of Lights
Hindu calendar, 5
Jewish calendar, 27

G

Gandhi, Indira, 147
Gandhi, Mohandas, 3, 6, 14
Hinduism and, 18–19
Ganesha, Hindu god, 12
Genesis, Sabbath tradition, 39
Ghost Festival, 51, 90
Golden Temple, Sikhism and, 147, 157
Good Friday, Christian holiday, 114
Gospel, Christianity, 115
Great Oneness school, Taoism, 62
Great Purity school, Taoism, 62
Guan Di (Guan Gong), 55
Guanyin, 83, 93
Gupta Empire, 3

Gurdwara Reform Movement, 147
Gurdwaras (sacred space),
Sikhism and, 148, 157
Gurpurbs, Sikh calendar, 148
Guru Granth Sahib, 146. *See also* Adi
Granth
Gyatso, Tenzin, 73, 84

H

Halal, Islamic dietary codes, 129, 130
Hanukkah
candles in menorahs, 38
Jewish calendar, 27
Hanuman, Hindu god, 12
Harappan Civilization, 3
Harmony, Taoism, 65
Hasidic Judaism, 25
Heavenly Mind school, Taoism, 62
Herzl, Theodor, 25
Hinduism, *x*
Brahman in, 7, 8–9
Buddha in, 76–77
Buddhism and, 92, 93
calendar of, 4–5
caste system and, 13–14
cheat sheet on, 2
Christianity and, 118
connections to other religions,
20–21
cows in, 15
daily puja, 11
evolution of, 2
founding of, 5–6
Gandhi and, 18–19
gods in, *xii*, 7–8, 10, 12
groups and sects within, 17
India and, 2, 3, 6, 14, 21
important figures within, 6
Judaism and, 44
karma in, 6–7
key dates, 3
leadership in, 17–18
"om" or "aum" symbol in, 19
parent religion to Buddhism, 1

reincarnation in, 7
sacred texts in, 12–13
Sikhism and, 164, 165
spiritual practices, 9–10
vegetarianism and, 14–15
yoga and, 16
Hitler, Adolf, 42
Holi, Hindu calendar, 4
Holika, Hindu demoness, 4
Holocaust, 23, 25
impact on Judaism, 41–43
Star of David, 40
Holy, defining the, *xi–xii*
Holy Bible, Christian text, 102
Holy war
jihad in Islam, 138–139
term, 139
Hukam (command), Sikh ritual, 154
Hungry Ghost Festival,
Taoist calendar, 51

I

Ik onkar, Sikh meditation, 162
Iliad (Homer), 13
Immortals, 55
India. *See* Buddhism; Hinduism;
Sikhism
Indus River Valley Civilization, 3, 5
Iscariot, Judas, 102
Islam, *x, xii*, 8
afterlife in, 141–142
beginning of, 126
beliefs and practices of,
131–132
Buddhism and, 93
calendar, 124
caliphs in, 140
call to prayer, 137
cheat sheet on, 122
China and, 143
Christianity and, 118, 119
crescent and star symbol in, 133
deity of, 128–129
dietary codes, 129, 130

Five Pillars of Islam, 131–132, 137
global religion, 121–122
Hinduism and, 21
Jesus and prophets, 140–141
jihad (holy war) in, 138–139
Judaism and, 44–45
key dates, 123
Khadija (Muhammad's wife), 127
Mecca, 127–128
monotheism, 118, 119, 121
Muhammad (Prophet), 121, 123, 125
poet Rumi and, 142
Quran, 135–136
Ramadan, 124
relating to other religions, 143
sacred spaces in, 132–133
sacred texts in, 134–135
Sikhism and, 164, 165
spread of, 138
Sunni and Shi'ite, 139–140
women's practices in, 136, 138
Islamic Sufism, 142, 156
Israel, importance to Jewish people, 43

J

Jade Emperor, Taoism, 55
Jainism, *xiv*, 76
ahimsa (noninjury), 15
karmain, 6
Sikhism and, 164
Jains, 5, 15, 162
Jehovah's Witnesses, 42
Jerusalem, Islam's holy
city, 128. *See also* Israel,
importance to Jewish people
Jesus, 95. *See also* Christianity; Islam
Christmas, 98
death of, 107–108
description of, 100
disciples of, 102–103
doctrine of Trinity, 101
Jewish Bible, 24, 30–31, 40
Christian Bible and, 31
The Jewish State (Herzl), 25

Jihad (holy war), Islam and, 138–139
Judaism, *x*, *xi*, 8
    Abraham and role in, 28–29
    afterlife in, 37–38
    bar mitzvah, 40
    cheat sheet on, 24
    Christianity and, 104, 106, 118–119
    connections to other
        religions, 44–45
    Conservative, 36, 38
    covenant, 23, 28, 30, 42
    deity of, 128–129
    founding of, 27–28
    Holocaust's impact on, 41–43
    homeland of Jewish people, 41
    importance of Israel to Jewish
        people, 43
    Islam and, 143
    Jewish Bible, 24, 30–31, 40
    Jewish calendar, 26–27, 38
    key dates, 25
    kosher codes, 33
    law for daily living, 32, 34
    messiah or savior figure, 36–37
    monotheism, 23–24, 27, 45, 68,
        118, 119
    Moses and role in, 29–30
    Orthodox Jews, 24, 32, 35, 36, 38
    parent religion of Christianity and
        Islam, 24
    Reform, 24, 36
    Sabbath observation, 39
    Talmud, 25, 31, 116
    temple and synagogue, 34–35
    Torah, 24, 25, 26, 30–32,
        39, 102, 116

K

Kabir (poet), 151
Kali, Hindu goddess, 12
Kamadhenu, Hindu goddess, 15
Kant, Immanuel, *xi*
Kantianism, *xi*

Karma. *See* Buddhism; Hinduism;
    Jainism; Sikhism
Ketuvim (Writings), Jewish Bible, 31
Khadija, Muhammad's wife, 127
Khalsa
    initiation, 153
    new names after initiation, 158
    Sikh division, 146, 161–162
    Sikh practice, 154
    sword-carrying, 153–154
    turban-wearing, 158–159
King, Martin Luther, Jr., 6, 19
Kosher codes
    Christianity on, 106–107
    halal codes by Islam, 129, 130
    Judaism, 33, 35, 36
Krishna, Hindu god, 12, 15
Kumbh Mela, Hindu calendar, 4

L

Lakshmi, Hindu goddess, 12
Langar (communal meal), Sikh ritual,
    154, 155
Lantern Festival, Taoist calendar, 50
Lao tzu, Taoism, 48, 49, 51–52, 53, 55, 57,
    65, 118–119
Laws of Manu (Manusmriti),
    Hindu text, 2
Lent, Christian calendar, 98, 114
Lotus flower, Buddhism and, 90
Luther, Martin, 97, 110

M

Mahabharata, Hindu text, 2, 3, 12–13
Maha Shivaratri, Hindu calendar, 4
Mahayana Buddhism, 72, 73, 80–81, 82,
    83, 89–90
Maimonides (Jewish scholar), 31
Mao, Chairman, *xiv*
Mecca, Islam's holy city, 127–128
Medina, Islam's holy city, 128
Meditation. *See also* Buddhism;
    Sikhism; Taoism
Mendelssohn, Moses, 25

Menorahs, Hanukkah, 38
Military Emperor (Guan Di), 55
Moksha (release), Hinduism, 7, 9
Monotheism
    Christianity, 101, 118–119
    Islam, 118, 119, 121
    Judaism, 23–24, 27, 45, 68, 118, 119
    Sikhism, 119, 145
Moses, 25
    death of, 106
    in Islam, 129
    role in Judaism, 29–30
    Ten Commandments, 28, 39
    Torah, 30
Mughal empire, *xiii*, 3, 21, 123, 140,
    147, 153
Muhammad (Prophet), 121, 123.
    See also Islam
    Islam founder, 125
    wife Khadija, 127
Mukti (spiritual liberation), Sikhism, 156
Muslims. *See* Islam
Mysticism, Sufi, 142, 156

N

Nanak, Sikhism and, 146–147, 149–151,
    155–156, 159–160
Navaratri, Hindu calendar, 5
Nazi Party, 25
Nevi'im (Prophetic books), Jewish
    Bible, 31
New Testament, 31, 102, 116
Nicene Creed, 101
Nichiren Buddhism, 73
Nirvana Day, Buddhist calendar, 74

O

Odyssey (Homer), 13
Old Testament, 24, 31, 102
Operation Blue Star, 147
Orthodox Christianity, 98, 102, 108,
    111, 112
Orthodox Jews, 24, 32, 35, 36, 38
Otto, Rudolf, *xi*

Ottoman empire, *xiii*, 41, 123
Ottomans, 25, 41, 123, 133, 140

P

Paath (reading), Sikh ritual, 154
Paranirvana, Buddhist calendar, 74
Parvati, Hindu goddess, 4
Passover, Jewish calendar, 26, 38
Patanjali (Hindu sage), 6, 16
Paul the Apostle, Christianity, 114–115
Pentateuch (five books), Torah, 30–31
Perfect Realization school, Taoism, 62
Pesach, Jewish calendar, 26
Protestantism, 108, 110–111, 113,
    117, 143
Protestant Reformation, 97, 102,
    110, 162
Puja, Hinduism, 11
Puranas, Hindu text, 12
Pure Land Buddhism, 73, 80, 83, 88

Q

Qi gong, everyday Taoism, 60
Quran
    caliphs of Islam, 135–136
    Jesus and prophets, 141

R

Rabbinic Judaism, 25
Ramadan, Islamic calendar, 124
Ramakrishna (Hindu mystic), 6
Ramayana, Hindu text, 2, 3, 12, 13
Rashi (Rabbi Solomon ben Isaac), 25, 31
Red Hats, Taoism, 61
Reform Judaism, 24, 36
Reincarnation
    in Buddhism, 79, 80
    in Hinduism, 7, 80
Religion, *ix*
    culture and, *x–xi*
    defining, *xi–xiii*
Roman Empire, 95, 101, 103–104, 111
Rosh Hashanah, Jewish calendar, 26
Rumi, Jalal ad-Din Muhammad, 123, 140
    and Shams al-Din, 142

S

Sabbath, Judaism and, 38, 39
Sadhu (Hindu holy man), 18
Sahajdharis, Sikh group, 146, 161
Samsara
  cycle of, 7, 9
  in Hinduism, 83
  lotus flowers symbol, 90
Sankaracharya, Adi (Sankara), 3, 6
Sant Movement, 147, 151
Saul (King), 25
Seder, 26
Shaivites, Hindu sect, 17
Shamanism, 57, 62
Shavuot, Jewish calendar, 26
Shield of David, 40
Shinto, *xiv*, 68, 71, 88
Shiva, Hindu god, 10
Shiva's Great Night, Hindu calendar, 4
Sikhism, *x*
  calendar, 148
  cheat sheet on, 146
  Christianity and, 119
  communal meal in, 155
  connections to major religions,
    164–165
  daily devotionals, 20, 160
  goal of spiritual practice, 156–157
  guru in, 150
  hair and physical appearance, 152
  Hindu and Muslim influences, 163
  Hinduism and, 20–21
  important gurus in, 151
  India and, 145
  Islam and, 143
  karmain, 6, 156, 163
  key dates, 147
  Khalsa initiation, 153
  khanda as symbol in, 159, 161
  main groups within, 161–162
  meditation, 154, 162
  monotheism, 119, 145, 162–163
  name origin of, 150
    names "Singh" and "Kaur", 158
    Nanak starting, 149
    sacred space of, 157–160
    scripture of, 151–152
    spread of, 159
    sword carrying in, 153–154
    turbans on men in, 158–159
    worship or practice in, 154, 156
Singh, Gobind, 147, 153
Solomon (King), 25, 34, 43
Spanish Inquisition, 25, 41
Spiritual regeneration, Sikhism,
  156–157
Star of David, 24, 38, 40
Stupas, Buddhism, 89
Sufism, Islamic, 142, 156
Sukkot, Jewish calendar, 27
Sundays, Christian "Sabbath", 105
Swami Vivekananda, 6, 18
Synagogue, Judaism, 34–35

T

Talmud, Judaism, 25, 31, 116
Tang dynasty, 49, 78, 82
Tantras, Hindu text, 12
Taoism, *x*
  alchemy in religious, 59
  Buddhism and, 93
  cheat sheet on, 48
  China and, 47–48, 56, 67
  Chuang tzu (Taoist master), 49,
    52-53, 57, 65
  Chuang tzu (Taoist text), 48, 49,
    52, 55
  Confucianism and, 65–66
  connections to other religions,
    67–68
  gods in, *xii*, 54, 55
  harmony as goal, 65
  Islam and, 143
  Judaism and, 44
  key dates, 49
  Lao tzu as leader, 48, 49, 51–52, 53,
    55, 57, 65, 118–119

leadership in, 59, 61
meditation, 59, 60, 67
name origin of, 53–54
philosophical, 57–58, 62–63, 65
practice of religious, 58–59
practice outside China, 66
priests functioning as shamans,
    61–62
qi gong, 60
religious, 57, 58, 62, 65
sacred spaces for, 58
Taoist calendar, 50–51
Tao Te Ching, 48, 49, 52, 55, 66
way/flow of all things, 64
yin and yang, 64
Tao Te Ching, Taoism, 48, 49, 52, 55, 66
Temple
    Judaism, 34–35
    Taoism, 56
Ten Commandments, 28, 39
Theravada Buddhism, 73, 81, 89
Three Caverns, Taoism, 48, 49, 55
Three Kings Day, Christian calendar, 98
Tomb Sweeping Day, Taoist calendar, 50
Torah
    in Jewish Bible, 30–31
    Judaism, 24, 25, 26, 32, 39, 102, 116
    Pentateuch, 30–31
Trinity
    Christian doctrine, 101
    Holy Spirit in, 115–116
    Muslims and, 129
Tripitaka (Three Baskets), Buddhist
    text, 72, 73, 84

U

Ulambana, Buddhist calendar, 90
Upanishads, Hindu text, 2, 3, 12

V

Vaisakhi, Sikh calendar, 148
Vaishnavites, Hindu sect, 17
Vajrayana Buddhism, 73, 83
Vedas, Hindu text, 2, 3, 12, 13
Vegetarianism

Buddhism, 90
Hinduism and, 14–15
Vesak (Buddha Day), Buddhist
    calendar, 74
Vishnu, Hindu god, 10

W

Western Wall, 35
White Cloud Monastery, Taoism, 62
William the Conqueror, 139

X

Xiayuan Festival, Taoist calendar, 51

Y

Yarmulke (kippah), 32
Yellow Emperor, Taoism, 55
Yin and yang, Taoism, 64, 66
Yoga
    Buddhism and, 85
    true roots of, 16
Yogacara school of Buddhism, 73
Yogis, Hinduism, 18
Yom Kippur, Jewish calendar, 26, 27, 38

Z

Zen Buddhism, 73, 82, 83, 88
Zionism, 40, 43
Zoroastrianism, *xiv*

ACKNOWLEDGMENTS

Thanks to the generous editors at Callisto Media for being so easy to work with and so helpful during the whirlwind process of writing this book. Special thanks to my family for filling in the childcare and general life maintenance gaps when I was on deadline. Finally, as always, I am forever grateful to Nishta Mehra, for being my "key" in life, and for 19 years of big talk about big ideas. I would not be the scholar or person I am without you.

ABOUT THE AUTHOR

 **Jill Carroll** earned her PhD in philosophy of religion from Rice University in Houston, Texas, and has taught world religions in university and community settings for 30 years. She provides religious diversity training for corporations and groups. She has given hundreds of talks and keynote addresses around the world on issues of religious tolerance and peaceful coexistence among people of all faiths and no faith. She currently lives in Phoenix, Arizona, with her wife and children.